Achieving QTS

Primary Mathematics: Audit and Test

Achieving QTS

Primary Mathematics: Audit and Test

Fourth edition

Mike Fletcher and Clare Mooney

Los Angeles | London | New Delhi
Singapore | Washington DC

Learning Matters
An imprint of SAGE Publications Ltd
1 Oliver's Yard
55 City Road
London EC1Y 1SP

SAGE Publications Inc.
2455 Teller Road
Thousand Oaks, California 91320

SAGE Publications India Pvt Ltd
B 1/I 1 Mohan Cooperative Industrial Area
Mathura Road
New Delhi 110 044

SAGE Publications Asia-Pacific Pte Ltd
3 Church Street
#10-04 Samsung Hub
Singapore 049483

Editor: Amy Thornton
Production controller: Chris Marke
Project management: Deer Park Productions, Tavistock, Devon
Marketing manager: Catherine Slinn
Cover design: Wendy Scott
Typeset by: C&M Digitals (P) Ltd, Chennai, India
Printed by: Henry Ling Limited at The Dorset Press, Dorchester, DT1 1HD

First published in 2001 by Learning Matters Ltd

Reprinted in 2002. Second edition published in 2003. Reprinted in 2003, 2004, 2005 and 2006. Third edition published in 2007. Reprinted in 2007 and 2008. Fourth edition published in 2014 by Sage/Learning Matters.

Library of Congress Control Number: 2013953924

British Library Cataloguing in Publication Data

A catalogue record for this book is available from the British Library

ISBN 978-1-4462-8271-7 (pbk)
ISBN 978-1-4462-8270-0 (hbk)

Contents

Introduction

About this book

This book has been written to support the subject knowledge learning of all primary trainee teachers on courses of Initial Teacher Training (ITT) in England and other parts of the UK where a secure subject knowledge and understanding of mathematics is required for the award of Qualified Teacher Status (QTS). A secure subject knowledge and understanding of mathematics is now widely acknowledged as a critical factor at every point in the complex process of planning, teaching and assessing mathematics. Indeed, Ma (1999) proposed that a *profound understanding of fundamental mathematics* is crucial to effective mathematics teaching. She suggested that teachers with a profound understanding of fundamental mathematics make connections between mathematical concepts and procedures from the simple to the complex and are knowledgeable about the whole primary mathematics curriculum, not just the content of a particular age level. This may well seem like a large a burden! However, persisting with the development of an appropriate level of mathematics subject knowledge will ensure confident mathematics teaching, motivating, challenging and extending the children.

The audit and test materials presented here are intended to help you to identify your own strengths and weaknesses in mathematics and to help you to set clear, appropriate and achievable targets for your own mathematical development:

Part 1 Mathematics background;

Part 2 Interest in mathematics;

Part 3 Perceived competence and confidence in mathematics;

Part 4 Mathematics test;

Part 5 Answers to test questions;

Part 6 Targets for further development;

Part 7 Revision and further reading.

It is quite likely that you will be required to undertake further auditing and testing of your subject knowledge and understanding of mathematics throughout your ITT course. You may wish to retain the audit and test results here for your own records and use them as working documents to return to as and when necessary. Your ITT provider may also wish to use them for their records.

You may indeed find the auditing and testing of your mathematics subject knowledge a daunting prospect, especially if you have not studied mathematics for several years. However, most people simply take it all in their stride and you should aim to do the same. Undertaking a self-audit and testing your own mathematical knowledge is just one part of the assessment process you will experience both during training and throughout your career in teaching. There is certainly nothing to worry about when auditing and testing yourself in the comfort of your own home, and your ITT provider will take every step it can to help you towards your goal of becoming an effective and successful primary school teacher.

For trainees wishing to undertake some revision or who feel the need for a mathematics study aid there are several excellent books written specifically for primary trainees with diverse backgrounds in mathematics, all available from good booksellers. The Learning Matters *Achieving QTS* series includes *Primary Mathematics: Knowledge and Understanding* (sixth edition) by Mooney et al. (2012; full details in References). Additional ideas for revision and further study are included in Part 7.

The Standards for Qualified Teacher Status (2012)

The *Professional Standards for Teachers* (TDA, 2012) provides a statutory framework for the career-long professional development of teachers designed by the Training and Development Agency for Schools (TDA). Within this wider framework, national standards are specified which trainee teachers must meet if they are to be awarded QTS.

These include, as aspects of professional knowledge and understanding, the requirements for trainee teachers to know and understand the National Curriculum for Mathematics and the Primary National Strategy Framework for Mathematics, and to have a secure knowledge and understanding of the mathematics curriculum as appropriate to the age range for which they are trained. The audit and test materials in this book include many aspects of the specific mathematics subject knowledge which you will need to know and understand in order to plan, teach and assess within these frameworks.

In terms of the professional skills set out in the standards, it is vital that your subject knowledge is sufficiently secure for you to feel confident in teaching and assessing children's learning. Strong subject knowledge will enable you to understand the concepts you teach so that you can explain them effectively and offer examples, and help your pupils to investigate them and develop their own understandings. The new curriculum requires pupils to understand Roman numerals and the binary system. This new edition includes examples of more difficult Roman numerals and an explanation of binary numbers. Strong subject knowledge will enable you to identify specifically what your pupils can do, and what they need to learn next. It will help you devise effective questions and provide feedback to move learning on. The new standards require teachers to 'foster and maintain pupils' interest in the subject'. Teachers will need, in addition to a sound subject knowledge, strategies to ensure that pupils find mathematics challenging and interesting. For example, when introducing Pythagoras' theorem to young children it is important that teachers are able to give practical examples of how Pythagoras' theorem is used in practice. A recent programme on television asked why Egyptian slaves building the pyramids carried a piece of string with 11 knots.

The string could be quickly made into a 3,4,5 triangle. 3,4,5 triangles are right angled, and this was a quick way to make a right angle and ensure that the pyramids were being built correctly. Teachers need to have examples like this to enthuse and motivate pupils.

The standards also require you to show that you are beginning to address your personal professional development through taking steps to identify and meet your own professional needs. This book, by helping you to identify particular areas of subject knowledge for further study, has been designed to help you do this. Where gaps in subject knowledge and understanding are identified, ITT providers are required to ensure that those areas needing attention are addressed and that, by the end of their course, trainees are both competent and confident in using their knowledge and understanding of mathematics in their teaching. An appropriate subject content for mathematics includes:

- **the real number system;**
- **indices;**
- **number operations and algebra;**
- **equations, functions and graphs;**
- **mathematical reasoning and proof;**
- **measures;**
- **shape and space;**
- **probability and statistics.**

The self-audit and test materials presented here will introduce you to the content items listed above in detail.

Mathematics: the statutory framework

The National Curriculum for England (2013)

So just what is it that all of this subject knowledge and understanding supports? In 1989 all maintained schools throughout England and Wales experienced the introduction of a National Curriculum for Mathematics (DfEE/QCA, 1999). Schools have a statutory duty to teach the National Curriculum. It is organised on the basis of four Key Stages, of which Key Stage 1 for 5–7 year-olds (Years 1 and 2) and Key Stage 2 for 7–11 year-olds (Years 3–6) cover the primary years. The components of each Key Stage include Programmes of Study, which set out the mathematics that children should be taught; Attainment Targets, which set out the mathematical knowledge, skills and understanding that children should attain; and Level Descriptions, which describe the types and range of performance that children working at a particular level should be able to demonstrate within each Attainment Target. A brief summary of Programmes of Study is presented as follows:

- **Using and applying mathematics;**
- **Number and algebra;**
- **Shape, space and measures;**
- **Handling data (Key Stage 2).**

The Foundation Stage

The scope of the National Curriculum was extended in 2002 to incorporate the Foundation Stage, introduced two years earlier as a distinct stage of education for children aged from 3 to 5. The Early Years curriculum, set out in *Curriculum Guidance for the Foundation Stage* (DfEE/QCA, 2000), covers six broad areas of learning, including 'Developing mathematical understanding and the foundations of numeracy'. Statutory early learning goals describe what children are expected to achieve in these areas by the end of the Reception year, and provide the basis for the Early Years curriculum. In autumn 2008, the Foundation Stage became part of the new Early Years Foundation Stage, covering care, learning and development for children in all Early Years settings from birth to the age of 5.

Mathematics: the non-statutory framework

The Primary National Strategy

The statutory Mathematics National Curriculum is fully supported by the Primary National Strategy's Primary Framework for Literacy and Mathematics, established in 2003 (see DfES, 2006). This national strategy brings both the National Numeracy Strategy and the National Literacy Strategy together. This framework is designed to offer a flexible structure to meet the learning needs of all children. Although schools are not legally required to use this framework, it interprets and develops the statutory curriculum, and is intended to promote progression and coherence from Reception year through to the end of primary schooling. A vast amount of associated guidance is available.

Many terms used in this book can be related directly to framework objectives and associated guidance materials, while others relate to concepts which will underpin your teaching of mathematics more generally.

References

DfEE/QCA (1999) *Mathematics: The National Curriculum for England*. London: HMSO. Available at www.nc.uk.net

DfEE/QCA (2000) *Curriculum Guidance for the Foundation Stage*. London: QCA.

DfES (2006) *Primary Framework for Literacy and Mathematics*. London: DfES. Available at http://www.standards.dfes.gov.uk/primaryframeworks/literacy/

Ma, L. (1999) *Knowing and Teaching Elementary Mathematics*. Mahwah, NJ: Lawrence Erlbaum.

Mooney, C. et al. (2012) *Primary Mathematics: Knowledge and Understanding* (6th edn). London: Sage/Learning Matters.

TDA (2012) *Standards for the Recommendation of Qualified Teacher Status*. London: TDA. Available at www.tda.gov.uk/

Part 1: Mathematics background

Provide as many background details as you can. Don't worry if it looks a bit 'blank' in places; you won't be alone.

▶ **personal details**

Name

Date of birth

Year(s) of course

Subject specialism

Elected Key Stage

▶ **mathematics qualifications**

GCSE/O level (equivalent)

Date taken

Grade(s)

GCE A level (equivalent)

Date taken

Grade(s)

▶ **mathematics degree**

Year of graduation

Class of degree

Other mathematics courses

▶ **other** (e.g. work related)

Part 2: Interest in mathematics

A positive attitude towards mathematics will help you to learn and teach it well, whether it is your favourite subject or not. Be honest with yourself and think carefully about your responses below. It is possible that you might have a healthy interest in mathematics even if you currently think you don't know much about it, and unfortunately the converse might be true!

Circle as appropriate using the key provided.

1 = I am very interested in mathematics.

2 = I am interested in mathematics.

3 = I am uncertain about my interest in mathematics.

4 = I am not interested in mathematics.

Interest **1**   **2**   **3**   **4**

A 1 or a 2 is fantastic, a 3 encouraging, a 4 well, you have yet to be inspired! Reflect critically on your attitude towards mathematics, positive or negative, and use the space below to comment further. Can you identify the experiences that gave rise to your interest or lack of interest in mathematics?

experiences statement

Part 3: Perceived competence and confidence in mathematics

As you undertake the following self-audit you might notice that you feel quite competent in an area of mathematics but lack the confidence to teach it. Competence and confidence are clearly quite different things. By the end of your training you will have greater competence within mathematics and greater confidence to teach the subject.

Competence

There are rather a lot of areas within this self-audit and you will need some time to read through and complete this part thoroughly. You do not need to know about or feel competent with everything listed here right now. This will develop throughout your training.

Please respond to the following statements using the key provided.

1 = **Very good. Existing competence perceived as *exceeding* the requirements.**

2 = **Good. Existing competence perceived as *meeting* the requirements *comfortably*.**

3 = **Adequate. Existing competence perceived as *meeting* the requirements but *some uncertainties* still exist.**

4 = **Not good. Existing competence perceived as *not meeting* the requirements.**

Number and algebra

a) the real number system	1	2	3	4
• the arithmetic of integers, fractions and decimals	1	2	3	4
• forming equalities and inequalities and recognising when equality is preserved	1	2	3	4
• the distinction between a rational number and an irrational number	1	2	3	4
• making sense of simple recurring decimals	1	2	3	4

b) indices

• representing numbers in index form including positive and negative integer exponents	1	2	3	4
• standard form	1	2	3	4

c) number operations and algebra

- using the associative, commutative and distributive laws   1   2   3   4
- use of cancellation to simplify calculations   1   2   3   4
- using the multiplicative structure of ratio and proportion to solve problems   1   2   3   4
- finding factors and multiples of numbers and of simple algebraic expressions   1   2   3   4
- constructing general statements   1   2   3   4
- Roman numerals and binary notation   1   2   3   4
- knowing when numerical expressions and algebraic expressions are equivalent   1   2   3   4
- number sequences, their nth terms and their sums   1   2   3   4

d) equations, functions and graphs

- forming equations and solving linear and simultaneous linear equations, finding exact solutions   1   2   3   4
- interpreting functions and finding inverses of simple functions   1   2   3   4
- representing functions graphically and algebraically   1   2   3   4
- understanding the significance of gradients and intercepts   1   2   3   4
- interpreting graphs, and using them to solve equations   1   2   3   4

Mathematical reasoning and proof   **1**   **2**   **3**   **4**

- the correct use of $=, \equiv, \Rightarrow, \therefore$ 1   2   3   4
- the difference between mathematical reasoning and explanation, as well as the proper use of evidence   1   2   3   4
- following rigorous mathematical argument   1   2   3   4
- familiarity with methods of proof, including simple deductive proof, proof by exhaustion and disproof by counter-example   1   2   3   4

Measures   **1**   **2**   **3**   **4**

- understanding that the basis of measures is exact and that practical measurement is approximate   1   2   3   4
- standard measures and compound measures, including rates of change   1   2   3   4
- the relationship between measures, including length, area, volume and capacity   1   2   3   4

- understanding the importance of choice of unit and use of proportion
  1   2   3   4

Shape and space

1   2   3   4

- Cartesian coordinates in 2-D
  1   2   3   4
- 2-D transformations
  1   2   3   4
- angles, congruence and similarity in triangles and other shapes
  1   2   3   4
- geometrical constructions
  1   2   3   4
- identifying and measuring properties and characteristics of 2-D shapes
  1   2   3   4
- using Pythagoras' theorem
  1   2   3   4
- recognising the relationships between and using the formulae for the area of 2-D shapes, including rectangle, triangle, trapezium, and parallelogram
  1   2   3   4
- the calculation of the area of circles and sectors, the length of circumferences and arcs
  1   2   3   4
- recognise, understand and use formulae for the surface area and volume of prisms
  1   2   3   4
- identifying 3-D solids and shapes and recognising their properties and characteristics
  1   2   3   4

Probability and statistics

1   2   3   4

- using discrete and continuous data and understanding the difference between them
  1   2   3   4
- tabulating and representing data diagrammatically and graphically
  1   2   3   4
- interpreting data and predicting from data
  1   2   3   4
- finding and using the mean and other central measures
  1   2   3   4
- finding and using measures of spread to compare distributions
  1   2   3   4
- using systematic methods for identifying, counting and organising events and outcomes
  1   2   3   4
- understanding the difference between probability and observed relative frequencies
  1   2   3   4
- recognising independent and mutually exclusive events
  1   2   3   4

Making sense of your perceived competence

Look back over the *perceived competency* grades within your self-audit. Summarise each area in the following table by looking at the distribution of responses. For example, if you ticked 1s, 2s and 3s in *The real number system* but no 4s, you should fill in your range as 1s to 3s. If you ticked more 3s than anything else, you should fill in your mode, the most frequently occurring response, as 3.

	range	mode
The real number system	_____	_____
Indices	_____	_____
Number operations and algebra	_____	_____
Equations, functions and graphs	_____	_____
Mathematical reasoning and proof	_____	_____
Measures	_____	_____
Shape and space	_____	_____
Probability and statistics	_____	_____

Mostly 1s　　Areas summarised as mostly 1s suggest that most competency requirements are exceeded. Your perceived competence would place you at a level beyond that indicated for a non-mathematics specialist. Well done.

Mostly 2s　　Areas summarised as mostly 2s suggest that most competency requirements are met comfortably. Some attention is necessary locally, certainly in weaker elements. Your perceived competence places you at a level about that of a non-mathematics specialist. With this sort of profile you probably have little to worry about.

Mostly 3s　　Areas summarised as mostly 3s suggest that most competency requirements are met adequately. However, attention is necessary throughout. Your perceived competence places you at a level best described as approaching that specified for a non-mathematics specialist. You are probably in good company, and with a little effort you will be up there with the best of them.

Mostly 4s　　Areas summarised as mostly 4s suggest that most competency requirements are hardly being met at all, but remember, you only have to get there by the end of your training, not before! Given the nature of the subject knowledge, a profile like this is not surprising. Consistent effort throughout your training will certainly result in a much improved competency profile, so don't worry.

Confidence

Carefully examine the Programmes of Study for Key Stages 1 and 2 in the Mathematics National Curriculum given below. Overall, how would you describe your confidence in terms of teaching them? Respond using the key provided.

1 = **Very good. Might even feel happy to support colleagues!**

2 = **Good. Further professional development required in some aspects.**

3 = **Adequate. Further professional development required in most aspects.**

4 = **Poor. Help! Further professional development essential in all aspects.**

Number and algebra

	1	2	3	4
• using and applying number	1	2	3	4
• numbers and the number system	1	2	3	4
• calculations	1	2	3	4
• solving numerical problems	1	2	3	4

Shape, space and measures

	1	2	3	4
• using and applying shape, space and measures	1	2	3	4
• understanding patterns and properties of shape	1	2	3	4
• understanding properties of position and movement	1	2	3	4
• understanding measures	1	2	3	4

Handling data (Key Stage 2)

	1	2	3	4
• using and applying handling data	1	2	3	4
• processing, representing and interpreting data	1	2	3	4

Making sense of your perceived confidence

1s and 2s are fantastic – what's kept you away from the profession for so long?! 3s are encouraging, and we would imagine many people would have this sort of profile. If you ticked any 4s, don't worry, you are being honest with yourself and that is good. If you felt so confident about teaching mathematics at this stage, it would be difficult to convince you that there was any point in training you to do it! Reflect critically on your perceived confidence about teaching mathematics and use the space below to comment further. Can you identify the 'source' of your confidence or of your lack of it?

confidence statement

Part 4: Mathematics test

Perceived competence and confidence is one thing. How would you do if actually put to the test? It really doesn't matter how well or how badly you do in the test now, you have lots of time to make up for the mathematics you have forgotten or never knew in the first place. The following pages explore your knowledge and understanding in the areas of mathematics identified in the self-audit in Part 3. Take as long as you need and try not to cheat too much by looking at the answers! The marking system is straightforward.

Number

1 Work out the following:

   (i) 5×24 (ii) 25×72 (iii) 312×235

   [3 MARKS]

2 Work out the following:

   (i) $1760 \div 40$ (ii) $1638 \div 63$ (iii) $3335 \div 23$

   [3 MARKS]

> **Key vocabulary** – algorithm, dividend, divisor, quotient, product

3 Using $p = \dfrac{2}{3}$, $q = \dfrac{1}{2}$, $r = 2\dfrac{4}{7}$ and $s = 1\dfrac{1}{5}$ find:

   (i) $p + q$ (ii) $p + r$ (iii) $q + s$
   (iv) $p - q$ (v) $r - q$ (vi) $r - s$
   (vii) $p \times q$ (viii) $q \times s$ (ix) $r \times s$
   (x) $p \div q$ (xi) $q \div p$ (xii) $q \div r$

   [12 MARKS]

> **Key vocabulary** – fraction, numerator, denominator, mixed fraction, vulgar fraction, vinculum

4 Convert the following into decimal fractions:

   (i) $\dfrac{5}{8}$ (ii) $\dfrac{7}{20}$ (iii)   65%   (iv)   0.1%

   [4 MARKS]

5 Convert the following to vulgar fractions:

   (i)   0.375   (ii)   0.28   (iii)   76%

   [3 MARKS]

6 Express the following vulgar fractions in their simplest forms:

(i) $\dfrac{84}{96}$ (ii) $\dfrac{84}{91}$

[2 MARKS]

7 Convert the following to percentages:

(i) $\dfrac{5}{8}$ (ii) 0.375   (iii) $\dfrac{7}{20}$

[3 MARKS]

Key vocabulary – equivalence, equivalent fraction, vulgar fraction, decimal fraction

8 Prior to Christmas the cost of the latest computer game was increased by 20%. In the sales after Christmas it was reduced by 20%. How do the two prices compare?

[1 MARK]

9 As it was so desirable, the cost of the latest mobile phone was increased by 25%. A month later it was no longer fashionable and was reduced by 20%. How did the reduced price compare with the original price before the increase?

[1 MARK]

10 A school basketball team scored 24 points in one game and 30 points in the next. What was their percentage increase in the points scored?

[1 MARK]

11 Two children undertake a sponsored swim. In total they raise £160. The ratio of the contributions of Edward to Katherine was 2:3. How much did each child raise?

[2 MARKS]

12 A junior school shares out library books to year groups based on the ratio of the number of children in the year groups. 1000 books are to be distributed to Years 3, 4, 5 and 6. There are 52 children in Year 3, 68 in Year 4, 44 in Year 5 and 36 in Year 6. How many books does each year group get?

[4 MARKS]

Key vocabulary – percentage, ratio, proportion

13 Place a tick in the box next to the numbers that are rational and a cross next to the numbers that are irrational.

(i)   0.3636363…   ☐   (ii) $\sqrt{2}$ ☐   (iii) $\sqrt{4}$ ☐

(iv) 0.101001000100001…   ☐   (v) π ☐   (vi) $\sqrt{8}$ ☐

(vii) 10π ☐   (viii) $\sqrt{2} \times \sqrt{8}$ ☐   (ix) $\sqrt{8} + \sqrt{8}$ ☐

[9 MARKS]

14 Place these numbers in numerical order:

| 71% | 5/7 | 18/25 | √1/2 | 0.7 |

[3 MARKS]

15 0.33333... can be written as 0.$\dot{3}$. Write the following recurring decimals using the same notation:

(i)   0.27272727...   (ii)   0.277777777...
(iii) 0.904904904904...   (iv)   18.181818...

[4 MARKS]

> **Key vocabulary**: rational number, irrational number, recurring decimal

16 Write these numbers in index form:

(i)   100 000   (ii)   0.1   (iii) 100

[3 MARKS]

17 Convert these numbers from standard form into ordinary form

(i) 6.6×10^3 (ii) 7.07×10^{-2}

[2 MARKS]

18 Write these numbers in standard form

(i)   523 000   (ii)   0.0606

[2 MARKS]

> **Key vocabulary**: index form, exponent, standard form

19 Put a tick in the box if the statement is **true** and a cross if the statement is **false**.

(i) $(24 + 8) \div 4 = (24 \div 4) + (8 \div 4)$ ☐

(ii) $32 \div (4 + 4) = (32 \div 4) + (32 \div 4)$ ☐

(iii) $12 \times (8 + 7) = (12 \times 8) + (12 \times 7)$ ☐

(iv) $(15 - 5) \times 10 = (15 \times 10) - (5 \times 10)$ ☐

(v) $(96 \div 12) \div 4 = 96 \div (12 \div 4)$ ☐

(vi) $(87 + 29) + 71 = 87 + (29 + 71)$ ☐

(vii) $40 - (30 - 10) = (40 - 30) - 10$ ☐

(viii) $(17 \times 4) \times 25 = 17 \times (4 \times 25)$ ☐

(ix) 17% of £50 = 50% of £17 ☐

(x) $(20 + 8) \times (30 + 9) = (20 \times 30) + (20 \times 9) + (8 \times 30) + (8 \times 9)$ ☐

[10 MARKS]

Mathematics test

20 Find all the factors of each of the following numbers:

    (i)   24   (ii) 360

[2 MARKS]

21 (i) What are the factors of 49?

    (ii) In general, what can you say about the number of factors of a square number?

[2 MARKS]

22 Express the following numbers in terms of their prime factors – for example, $44 = 2 \times 2 \times 11$:

    (i)   48   (ii) 105   (iii)   36   (iv)   56

[4 MARKS]

23 Find the highest common factor of each of the following:

    (i)   36 and 48   (ii) 105 and 56

    (iii) a^2b^2 and a^3b (iv) abc and cd^3

[4 MARKS]

24 Write the following Roman numbers using Hindu-Arabic notation.

    (i)   DCCCLXXXVIII
    (ii) MCMXCIX
    (iii) MMCCXX

[3 MARKS]

25 Express the following Hindu-Arabic numbers using Roman notation.

    (i)   333
    (ii)   444
    (iii) 2013

[3 MARKS]

26 Write the following numbers using numerals:

    (i)   Thirty seven thousand two hundred and three
    (ii) Two hundred and three million one thousand and fifty
    (iii) Nine million and seventeen

[3 MARKS]

27 Write the following numbers in words

    (i)   40404040
    (ii) 70007007
    (iii) 300030003

[3 MARKS]

28 What are the answers to the following calculations when (a) a primary calculator (b) a scientific calculator is used? (Note: primary calculators have no order of precedence. If 5 + 2 × 3 = is punched into a primary calculator the display will read 21. Scientific calculators have an order of precedence. If 5 + 2 × 3 = is punched into a scientific calculator the display will read 11.)

(i) $7 + 2 \times 3$
(ii) $8 \div 2 + 2$
(iii) $8 + 2 \div 2$
(iv) $5 \times 5 + 3$
(v) $2 + 3 \times 5 - 1$
(vi) $3 + 6 \div 3 + 3$
(vii) $3 + \sqrt{16} \times 4$
(viii) $8 \div 2 + 4 \div 2$
(ix) $8 \times 4 \div 2$
(x) $16 + 4 \div 2 \div 2$

[20 MARKS]

29 Change the following binary numbers into base ten numbers.

(i)   111
(ii)   1110

[2 MARKS]

30 Change the following base ten numbers into binary numbers.

(i)   24
(ii)   48

[2 MARKS]

Algebra – patterns and relationships

1 If $a = 5$, $b = 15$, $c = 2$, $d = 3$, $de = 15$ and $df = 18$ find:

(i)	ab	(ii)	ac	(iii)	e
(iv)	f	(v)	$a(b + c)$	(vi)	$d(e + f)$
(vii)	$a(b - c)$	(viii)	$d(e - f)$	(ix)	$2a^2b$
(x)	$2d^2e$	(xi)	$\dfrac{1}{a}$	(xii)	$\dfrac{1}{d}$

[12 MARKS]

2 Liam is doing a mathematics investigation and obtains the results 1, 4, 9, 16, 25.

(i) What would be the next term in this sequence?

[1 MARK]

(ii) The 10th term?

[1 MARK]

(iii) The nth term?

[2 MARKS]

3 Winston is investigating the number of slabs that would be required to pave around a square garden pond as follows:

pond 1

pond 2

pond 3

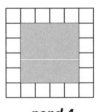
pond 4

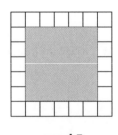
pond 5

(i) Write down the number pattern that he found.

[1 MARK]

(ii) How many slabs would be needed to pave around the 10th pond?

[1 MARK]

(iii) What would be the nth term of this sequence?

[2 MARKS]

4   Katy is doing a mathematics investigation and obtained the results 1, 2, 4, 8, 16, 32.

   (i)   What would be the next term in this sequence?

[1 MARK]

   (ii)   The 10th term?

[1 MARK]

   (iii)   The nth term?

[2 MARKS]

5   Anoushka is investigating multilink staircases as follows:

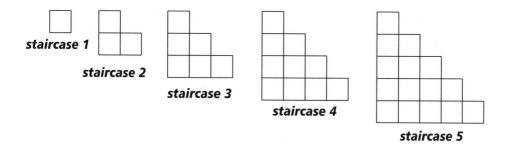

staircase 1

staircase 2

staircase 3

staircase 4

staircase 5

   (i)   Write down the number pattern that she found.

[1 MARK]

   (ii)   How many cubes would be needed for the 10th staircase?

[1 MARK]

   (iii)   What would be the nth term of this sequence?

[2 MARKS]

Key vocabulary: generalise, nth term, number sequence, investigation, triangle numbers, square numbers, geometric series

6   Solve the following equations:

   (i) $\dfrac{1}{x+2} = 3$

   (ii) $\dfrac{1}{5x-4} = \dfrac{1}{x}$

   (iii) $\dfrac{3}{1+b} = \dfrac{5}{b+3}$

[3 MARKS]

Key vocabulary: solve, equation

7   Solve the following pairs of simultaneous equations. Find x and y in each case:

(i) $\begin{cases} y - 2x = 4 \\ y + x = 7 \end{cases}$

(ii) $\begin{cases} 2x - 3y = 2 \\ 4x + 6y = 4 \end{cases}$

(iii) $\begin{cases} 2x - y = 5 \\ 3x + 2y = 11 \end{cases}$

[6 MARKS]

8   In which of the equations is there a unique real solution for x? Explain your reasoning.

(i) $x^2 = -4$

(ii) $3(x + 2) = 3x + 6$

(iii) $3(x + 2) = 2x + 8$

[6 MARKS]

Key vocabulary: simultaneous equations, imaginary number, real number, identity

9   Which of the following statements are true and which are false?

(i)   If $x > 3$ then $x^2 > 9$

(ii)   If $x < -4$ then $x^2 < 16$

(iii)   If $3x > -12$ then $x > -4$

(iv)   If $x/2 < 6$ then $x < 12$

(v)   If $x > 2$ then $x^3 > 8$

(vi)   If $x < -3$ then $x^3 < -27$

(vii)   If $6 - x > 10$ then $x > 4$

[7 MARKS]

Shape and space

1 If angle *a* is 100°, work out angles *b, c, d, e* and *f*.

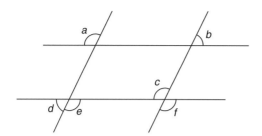

[1 MARK]

2 If angle *a* = 95°, angle *b* = 110° and angle *c* = 105°, what does angle *d* equal?

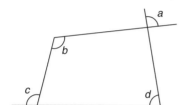

[1 MARK]

Key vocabulary: opposite angles, complementary angles, supplementary angles, interior angles

3

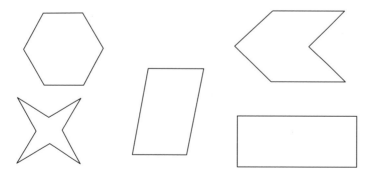

(i)   Identify the lines of symmetry of the shapes above.

[5 MARKS]

(ii)   Identify the orders of rotational symmetry of the shapes above.

[5 MARKS]

Key vocabulary: reflective symmetry, order of rotational symmetry

21

4 Identify which of the angles in the following shape are acute, obtuse, right or reflex.

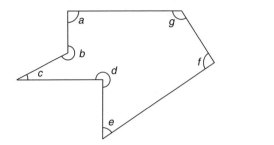

angle a:

angle b:

angle c:

angle d:

angle e:

angle f:

angle g:

[7 MARKS]

Key vocabulary: acute angle, right angle, obtuse angle, reflex angle

5

(i)   Which of these shapes are congruent?

[2 MARKS]

(ii)   Which of these shapes are similar to shape C?

[2 MARKS]

Key vocabulary: congruence, similarity, transformations

6 Fill in the blanks:

A regular triangle is called an _____ triangle. Because it is a regular polygon it is clear that all the sides are of _____ and all the angles are the same size, i.e. _____ o.

Again because an _____ triangle is regular it has _____ lines of reflective symmetry and rotational symmetry of order _____.

A triangle which has two sides of equal length is called an_____ triangle. As well as having two sides of equal length an _____ triangle also has __ angles of equal size. An_____ triangle has_____ line of reflective symmetry and rotational symmetry of order_____.

A triangle which has three sides of different length and no equal angles is called a _____triangle. _____ triangles have_____ lines of reflective symmetry and rotational symmetry of order_____ .

A triangle containing one angle of 90° is called a _____-_____ triangle. A_____-_____ triangle will be either an_____ or_____ triangle. A right-angled triangle cannot be _____.

The number of lines of reflective symmetry of a _____-_____ triangle depends on whether it is an_____ or_____ triangle.

A triangle with an obtuse angle cannot be _____-_____.

[24 MARKS]

Key vocabulary: triangle, equilateral, isosceles, scalene, right-angled, reflective symmetry, rotational symmetry, obtuse

7 Put a tick in the box if the following triangles have right angles:

(i)   AB = 3   BC = 4   AC = 5

(ii) XY = 4   YZ = 5   XZ = 6

[2 MARKS]

Key vocabulary: Pythagoras' theorem, right angle

8 What is the area of this triangle?

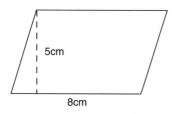

5cm

3cm

4cm

[1 MARK]

9 What is the area of this parallelogram?

5cm

8cm

[1 MARK]

23

10 What is the area of this trapezium?

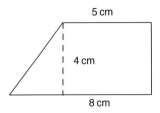

[1 MARK]

11 Work out the perimeter and area of the following shape:

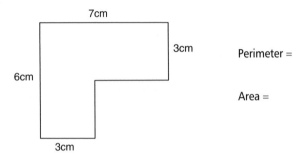

Perimeter =

Area =

[2 MARKS]

12 Work out the perimeter and area of the following shape (you will need to calculate *L* using Pythagoras' theorem).

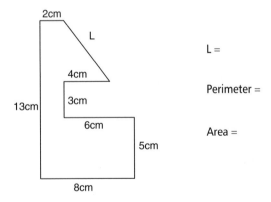

L =

Perimeter =

Area =

[3 MARKS]

Key vocabulary: perimeter, area, parallelogram, trapezium, triangle

13 Find the circumference and area of a circle with a diameter of 10 cm.

[2 MARKS]

14

Circle A

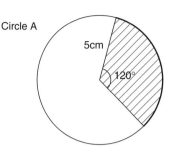

5cm
120°

Circle B

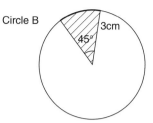

3cm
45°

(i) Calculate the area of the sector marked in each circle.

[2 MARKS]

(ii) Calculate the length of the arcs marked on each circle above.

[2 MARKS]

Key vocabulary: radius, diameter, circumference, area, sector, arc

15 This rectangle has the following coordinates:

a (1, 1)
b (1, 3)
c (5, 3)
d (5, 1)

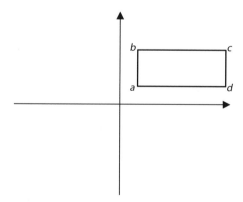

Work out the new coordinates when the rectangle is:

(i) reflected in the *y*-axis;
(ii) rotated 90 degrees clockwise about the point (0,0).

[8 MARKS]

Key vocabulary: Cartesian coordinates, reflection, rotation

16 Name the *five* Platonic solids. What links the solids in this group?

[6 MARKS]

17 Draw *two* different nets for a tetrahedron.

[2 MARKS]

18 Draw three different nets for a cube.

[3 MARKS]

19 Identify the number of faces, vertices and edges on the following solids:

Solid	Faces	Edges	Vertices
Cube	_____	_____	_____
Tetrahedron	_____	_____	_____
Triangular prism	_____	_____	_____

[9 MARKS]

Key vocabulary: face, edge, vertex, net, Platonic solid, cube, tetrahedron, prism

20 A cuboid has edges of lengths 3 cm, 4 cm and 6 cm.

    (i)   What is the area of each face?   [3 MARKS]

    (ii)   What is the total surface area of the cuboid?   [1 MARK]

    (iii) What is the volume of the cuboid?   [1 MARK]

21 Find the surface area and volume of the following cylinder, with radius 5 cm and length 10 cm.

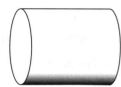

Surface area =

Volume =

[2 MARKS]

22 Find the surface area and volume of the following triangular prism:

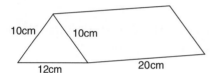

Surface area =

Volume =

[2 MARKS]

Key vocabulary: surface area, volume, cuboid, cylinder, prism

---

23 Which of the following statements are true and which are false? Explain your reasoning.

    (i)   An octahedron is a prism.

    (ii)   It is possible for a polyhedron to have 9 faces, 9 vertices and 16 edges and not be a pyramid.

    (iii) A cuboid is a prism.

    (iv) A dodecahedron has 20 faces.

    (v)   An icosahedron has 12 vertices.

    (vi) An octahedron has 6 vertices.

    (vii) A cube has 12 edges.

    (viii) It is possible for a polyhedron to have 7 faces, 7 vertices and 12 edges.

    (ix) A tetrahedron has three planes of symmetry.

    (x)   It is possible for a polyhedron to have 5 faces.

[20 MARKS]

Statistics

1   Find the mode, median and mean of the data set:

3   3   3   3   3   3   4   5   5   6   6

[3 MARKS]

2   The average adult male shoe size is size 8.

The average salary in the United Kingdom is £21500

The sign in a lift says 'Maximum number of occupants 6. Average weight of occupants 80 kg.'

For each of the above determine which average is being referred to: the mode, median or mean.

[3 MARKS]

3   Find the lower quartile, median, upper quartile, range and inter-quartile range of the data set:

2   3   3   4   6   6   7   8   9   10   11

[5 MARKS]

4   Alf, Bill and Khalid are cricketers. Each player has played 10 times this year. The table shows the range and mean of the number of runs scored by each player.

	Range	Mean
Alf	40	40
Bill	10	45
Khalid	20	45

(i)   Which player scored the least runs in total?
(ii)   Which player is the most consistent?
(iii) One of the players scored 66 runs in one of his innings. Who was this?
(iv) One of the players' lowest score was 24 runs. Who was this?

[4 MARKS]

5   Find the modes, median and mean of this data set.

2   2   2   3   4   5   5   5   6   6

[4 MARKS]

> **Key vocabulary**: mode, median, mean, range, lower quartile, upper quartile, inter-quartile range, bimodal

6   The scatter diagram shows the actual ages and reading ages of the pupils in a class.

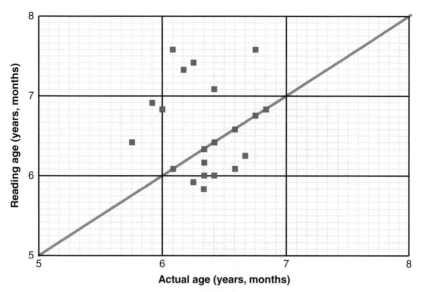

(i)   How many pupils are there in the class?
(ii)   How many pupils have the same reading age as their chronological age?
(iii)   Identify the pupil who has the greatest difference between their reading age and their actual age.

[3 MARKS]

7   A teacher gave two tests to his class of pupils. The results are shown in the dual bar chart.

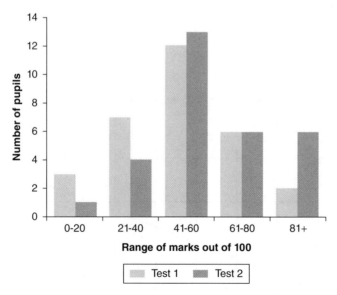

(i)   How many pupils are there in the class?
(ii)   How many pupils scored more than 40 marks in test 1?
(iii)   How many pupils scored fewer than 81 marks in test 2?
(iv)   Is the mean mark higher in test 1 or test 2?

[4 MARKS]

29

8   The pie chart shows how pupils travelled to school.

82 came by car, 14 cycled, 38 walked and 48 came by bus.

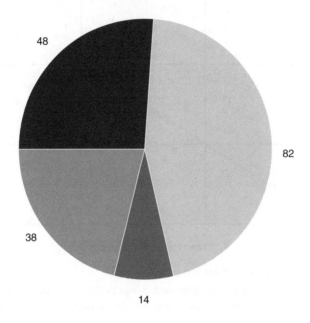

Which of the following statements are true? Explain your reasoning.

(i)   3/7 came by car
(ii) 1/13 cycled
(iii) 2/7 walked

[6 MARKS]

9   Use the conversion graph to answer the questions.

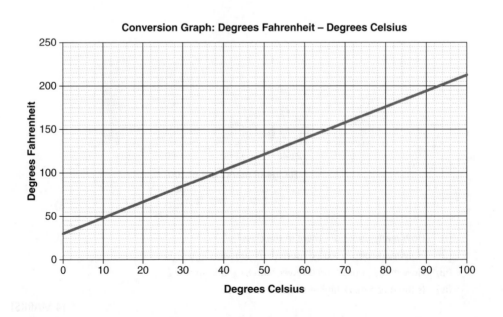

(i)   Change 10 degrees Celsius into degrees Fahrenheit.

(ii) Which is hotter 40 degrees Celsius or 100 degrees Fahrenheit?

(iii) Water boils at 212 degrees Fahrenheit. At how many degrees Celsius does water boil?

[3 MARKS]

Key vocabulary: scatter diagram, dual bar chart, pie chart, conversion graph

10 Categorise the following variables as either discrete, continuous or categoric:

(i)   Eye colour

(ii) Shoe size

(iii) Type of breakfast cereal

(iv) Height

(v)   Weight

[5 MARKS]

Key vocabulary: discrete, continuous, categoric

Probability

1 Dice are numbered 1–6. Two fair dice are thrown and the numbers added. Find the probability that the total is:

    (i)   2   (ii)   7   (iii) 6   (iv) 14

[4 MARKS]

2   (i)   A fair die is rolled. What is the probability that a 5 will be rolled?
     (ii) A coin is flipped. What is the probability tails is uppermost?
     (iii) A fair die is rolled and a coin is flipped. What is the probability of a 5 showing on the die and tails on the coin?

[3 MARKS]

3 A card is drawn from a pack of 52. What is the probability:

      (i)   it is a heart?
      (ii) it is a black card?
      (iii) it is a card less than a 10? (Ace is high.)
      (iv) that the card is higher than a Jack? (Ace is high.)

[4 MARKS]

4 A card is drawn at random from a pack of 52 playing cards and turned over. It is the Jack of Spades.

What is the probability the next card drawn is:

      (i)   a card higher than a Jack?
      (ii) a card lower than a Jack?
      (iii) a Jack?

(Ace is high.)   [3 MARKS]

5 In a TV game show a card is drawn at random from a pack of 52 playing cards. A contestant then has to guess if the next card drawn will be higher or lower than his starting card. (Ace is high.)

      (i)   What is the worst card that the contestant could start with?   [1 MARK]
      (ii) What are the best cards a contestant could start with?   [2 MARKS]

6 Asif has the following cards:

21 ☹	30 ☺	15 ☹	39 ☺	18 ☺	34 ☹	42 ☺	27 ☺

      (i)   Gareth takes a card without looking. He says, 'I'm more likely to have an even number than an odd number'. Is he correct? Explain.

[1 MARK]

(ii) Choose one of the following words to complete the sentences below.

likely   impossible   certain   unlikely

a) It is _____ that Gareth's card will contain ☹
b) It is _____ that Gareth's number will be greater than 10.

[2 MARKS]

Key vocabulary: probability, conditional probability, impossible, certain, likely, unlikely

7   Which of the following are true and which are false? Explain your reasoning.

(i)   If two coins are thrown the probability of two heads landing upwards is 1/3.
(ii)   If two six-faced dice are thrown the probability the total is 12 is 1/36.
(iii) Two cards are dealt from a pack of 52 playing cards. The probability they are both hearts is 1/16.
(iv) Two cards are dealt from a pack of 52 playing cards. The probability they are both black is less than ¼.
(v)   Two tetrahedral dice, numbered 1 to 4, are thrown. The probability the sum of the two numbers on the lower faces is 8 is 1/16.

[10 MARKS]

Key vocabulary: independent and dependent events

Measures

1 Metric: metre, hectare, square centimetre, tonne, litre, kilogram, cubic centimetre, gram, kilometre, centimetres per minute, centimetres per year, kilometres per hour

Imperial: ton, pint, pound, cubic inch, ounce, yard, acre, mile, square inch, miles per hour, inches per minute, inches per year

For each of the following choose the appropriate measure from the list above. Choose an Imperial measure and a metric measure in each case.

    (i)   The length of a football pitch

    (ii) The mass of a baby

    (iii) The distance from London to Brighton

    (iv) The area of a piece of A4 paper

    (v)   The area of a farmer's field

    (vi) The mass of a bag of sweets

    (vii) The capacity of a large bottle

    (viii) The mass of a bus

    (ix) The speed of a car

    (x)   The speed of a snail

    (xi) The speed at which hair grows

    (xii) The volume of a match box

[24 MARKS]

2 Identify which is bigger.

    (i)   Acre or hectare

    (ii)   Litre or 2 pints

    (iii)   Kilogram or 2 pounds

    (iv)   Yard or metre

    (v)   Mile or 2 kilometres

    (vi)   Gallon or 3 litres

    (vii) Inch or 2 centimetres

    (viii) 4 furlongs or 1 kilometre

[8 MARKS]

Key vocabulary: Imperial measure, metric measure

3 A map has a scale of 1:50000. What do the following distances on the map represent?

    (i)   1 centimetre

    (ii)   1 millimetre

[2 MARKS]

4 Identify the scale of a map if 2 centimetres on the map represents 2 kilometres.

What distance on this map represents:

(i)   10 kilometres?

(ii)   100 metres?

[2 MARKS]

5 Identify the scale of a map if

(i)   1 centimetre represents 100 metres.

(ii)   1 metre represents 10 kilometres.

(iii)   1 millimetre represents 100 metres.

[3 MARKS]

Key vocabulary: scale, ratio

6 Change the following into kilometres per hour:

(i)   10 metres per second

(ii)   100 metres per minute

(iii)   50 centimetres per second

[3 MARKS]

7 Which two of the following does a newton measure?

Mass, weight, force, velocity, acceleration, speed, power.   [2 MARKS]

8 Which of the following is a megabit per second?

(i) 10^6 bits per second

(ii) 10^{12} bits per second

(iii) 10^3 bits per second

[1 MARK]

Key vocabulary: compound measure, newton

9 How many days are there from:

(i)   23 April until 18 September?

(ii)   1 February 2014 until 1 August 2014?   [2 MARKS]

10 How many leap years are there between 1890 and 2018?   [1 MARK]

11 How long is it from:

    (i)   9.32 a.m. until 3.18 p.m.

    (ii)   07.35 until 18.48

[2 MARKS]

Key vocabulary: leap year, 24 hour clock, a.m., p.m.

12 Which of the following are true and which are false? Explain your reasoning.

    (i)   A size 8 shoe is twice as long as a size 4 shoe.

    (ii)   An oven setting of 6 is twice as hot as an oven setting of 3.

    (iii) A size 48 (continental size) shoe is twice as long as a size 24 (continental size) shoe.

    (iv) A wind speed of 8, on the Beaufort scale, is twice that of a wind speed of 4 on the Beaufort scale.

    (v)   An earthquake measuring 8 on the Richter scale is twice as powerful as one measuring 4.

    (vi) A temperature of 40 degrees Celsius is twice as hot as a temperature of 20 degrees Celsius.

    (vii) An electric appliance that uses 10 amps of current is using twice as much electricity as one that uses 5 amps of current.

    (viii) A car that travels at 100 km/hr is travelling twice as fast as one that travels at 50 km/hr.

    (ix) A man with a mass of 100 kg is twice as heavy as someone with a mass of 50 kg.

    (x)   An A4 piece of paper is twice the size of an A2 piece of paper.

[20 MARKS]

Key vocabulary: ratio scale, interval scale, geometric scale

Equations and graphs

1 Linda is setting out from home for a bike ride. The distance–time graph shows the journey.

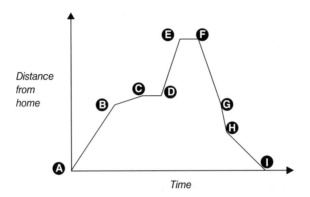

(i) Which part of the graph shows Linda cycling up a steep hill?

[1 MARK]

(ii) Which parts of the graph show her having a rest?

[2 MARKS]

(iii) Which point on the graph shows her arriving home?

[1 MARK]

(iv) Which part of the graph shows her cycling down a steep hill?

[1 MARK]

(v) Was Linda travelling faster on the DE section of the journey or the FG section of her journey?

[1 MARK]

(vi) Was she travelling faster on the AB section of her journey or the DE section of her journey?

[1 MARK]

(vii) Was she travelling faster on the AB section of her journey or the HI section of her journey?

[1 MARK]

(viii) The time spent travelling was greater than the time spent resting. True or false?

[1 MARK]

2   This is the graph of y = 10x + 8.

What is:

    (i)   the gradient of the line?

    (ii)   the y-intercept?

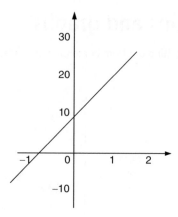

[2 MARKS]

3   Write down the equation of the following graph:

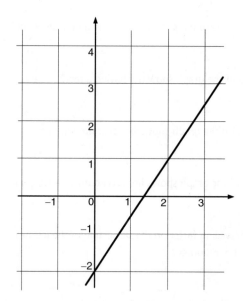

[1 MARK]

4   Write down the gradient and y-intercept of each of the following graphs of linear equations:

    (i) $y = \dfrac{2}{3}x + 6$ Gradient =

                                   y-intercept =

    (ii) 2y = 3x − 6   Gradient =

                                   y-intercept =

[4 MARKS]

5 Which four of the following equations are equivalent to the linear equation $2x - 3y = 24$?

(i) $y = 2x/3 - 8$
(ii) $x = 24 - 3y/2$
(iii) $24 = -3y + 2x$
(iv) $y = 2x/3 + 8$
(v) $3y + 24 = 2x$
(vi) $x = 12 + 3y/2$
(vii) $12 = x - 2y/3$

[4 MARKS]

Key vocabulary: distance-time graph, gradient, y-intercept, linear equation

6 Which of the following are linear equations and which are non-linear equations? A linear equation will give a straight-line graph when it is plotted. A non-linear equation will not give a straight-line graph when it is plotted. Explain your reasoning.

(i) $x + y = 10$
(ii) $xy = 10$
(iii) $x - y = 10$
(iv) $x/y = 10$
(v) $2x + 3y = 12$
(vi) $y = 6 - x$
(vii) $y = x^2$
(viii) $y = 4/x$
(ix) $y = x/4$
(x) $x = 4/y$

[20 MARKS]

Key vocabulary: linear equation, non-linear equation

Reasoning and proof

1   Say whether the following statements are true or false. Explain your reasoning.

    (i)   The product of two consecutive numbers is always divisible by 2. (Note: the product of 3 and 4 is 12.)

    (ii)   The sum of three consecutive numbers is always even.

    (iii)   The product of three consecutive numbers is always divisible by 6.

    (iv)   The sum of four consecutive numbers is always even.

    (v)   An odd number minus an odd number is an odd number.

    (vi)   An odd number multiplied by an odd number is an odd number.

    (vii)   The sum of four consecutive numbers is never divisible by 4.

    (viii) The sum of five consecutive numbers is always divisible by 5.

[16 MARKS]

2   Which of the following are true and which are false? (*x* is a real number.)

    (i) $2(x + 4) = 2x + 8$

    (ii) $3(x - 3) = 3x - 6$

    (iii) $x^2 = -9$

[3 MARKS]

3   Prove that there are exactly four prime numbers between 10 and 20.

[1 MARK]

4   Prove that the sum of any two odd numbers is even.

[1 MARK]

5   Show that when two six-faced dice are thrown a total of 6 is more likely than a total of 4.

[1 MARK]

6   The triangle numbers are: 1 3 6 10 15 21 28 36 45 55 66 ...

What do you notice about the sum of any two consecutive triangle numbers?

Explain why this happens. [2 MARKS]

7   The square numbers are: 1 4 9 16 25 36 49 64 81 ...

What do you notice about the difference between consecutive square numbers?

Explain why this happens.

[2 MARKS]

8 Which of the following statements are true and which are false?

(i) All squares are rectangles.

(ii) If a shape is both a rectangle and a rhombus then it is a square.

(iii) If a shape is a rectangle then it is a parallelogram.

(iv) If a shape is a parallelogram then it is a rhombus.

[4 MARKS]

Key vocabulary: prove, show, explain, deductive proof, proof by exhaustion, disproof by counter-example, if, then

Making sense of your test results

How well did you do? Determine a separate percentage score for each area, and then determine an overall score for the test. Remember that your percentage score is relative to the nature of the material tested and the time at which the test took place.

			Score		Percentage
Number	Marks _____	(max. 120)		_____ %
Algebra	Marks _____	(max. 50)		_____ %
Shape and space	Marks _____	(max. 120)		_____ %
Statistics	Marks _____	(max. 40)		_____ %
Probability	Marks _____	(max. 30)		_____ %
Measures	Marks _____	(max. 70)		_____ %
Equations and graphs	Marks _____	(max. 40)		_____ %
Reasoning and proof	Marks _____	(max. 30)		_____ %
Overall	Marks _____	(max. 500)		_____ %

Consider the following divisions against which your separate and overall test scores can be measured. The scale is based upon our experiences of testing trainees in this way. It should be used for guidance and to aid target setting and not taken as some sort of absolute test measure.

80–100%	In the areas tested, your score is very good and indicates that you exceed the level expected of a non-mathematics specialist. Well done.
60–80%	In the areas tested, your score is good and indicates that you meet the level expected of a non-mathematics specialist. Some attention is necessary in weaker questions.
50–60%	In the areas tested, your score is adequate and indicates that you are moving towards the level expected of a non-mathematics specialist.
0–50%	In the areas tested, your score is low. Use the test positively to target the areas you need to work on. Remember, you only have to get there by the end of your training.

A useful tip would be to take a break from testing for now. Use the test questions as a guide for some revision (see Part 7 for further recommendations). Come back to the different sections of the test later and see how much progress you have made.

Part 5: Answers to test questions

Number

1 (i)   This can be solved mentally. Multiplying by 5 is the same as multiplying by 10 and dividing by 2.

120 is the product.

(ii)   This can be solved mentally. Multiplying by 25 is the same as multiplying by 100 and dividing by 2 and dividing by 2 again.

1800 is the product.

(iii) $312 \times 235 = 73\,320$

This problem needs to be solved by using a long multiplication algorithm.

```
     312
 ×   235
    1560
    9360
   62400
   73320
   1 1 1
```

2 (i)   This problem can be solved without using an algorithm.

The dividend, 1760, and the divisor, 40, have a common factor of 10.
$1760 \div 40$ is the same as $176 \div 4$.
To divide by 4 we half and half again.
The quotient is 44.

(ii)   This problem can be solved without using an algorithm.

The dividend,1638, and the divisor, 63, have a common factor of 9. (Note also that 1638 is divisible by 9 because its digits add up to 18 which is divisible by 9.)

```
      1 8 2
 9)16⁷3¹8
```

$1638 \div 63$ is the same as $182 \div 7$.

The quotient is 26.

(iii)   3325 and 23 have no factors in common. This problem needs to be solved by using a long division algorithm.

$3335 \div 23 = 145$

```
      1  4  5
 23)33¹⁰3¹¹5
```

Many schools teach pupils the 'chunking method' to solve division problems. This approach is popular in Holland and some other European countries.

```
3335
2300    100          (23 × 100 = 2300)
1035                 (3325 – 2300 = 1035)
 920     40          (23 × 40 = 920)
 115                 (1035 – 920 = 115)
 115      5          (23 × 5 = 115)
```

So the answer is 100 + 40 + 5 = 145

3 (i) $p + q = \dfrac{2}{3} + \dfrac{1}{2} = \dfrac{4}{6} + \dfrac{3}{6} = \dfrac{7}{6} = 1\dfrac{1}{6}$

7/6 is a vulgar fraction. A fraction consisting of a whole number and a vulgar fraction is called a mixed fraction. The top line of a fraction is called the numerator. The bottom line is called the denominator. The line separating the numerator and the denominator is the vinculum or fraction bar.

(ii) $p + r = \dfrac{2}{3} + 2\dfrac{4}{7} = \dfrac{2}{3} + \dfrac{18}{7} = \dfrac{14}{21} + \dfrac{54}{21} = \dfrac{68}{21} = 3\dfrac{5}{21}$

(iii) $q + s = \dfrac{1}{2} + 1\dfrac{1}{5} = \dfrac{1}{2} + \dfrac{6}{5} = \dfrac{5}{10} + \dfrac{12}{10} = \dfrac{17}{10} = 1\dfrac{7}{10}$

(iv) $p - q = \dfrac{2}{3} - \dfrac{1}{2} = \dfrac{4}{6} - \dfrac{3}{6} = \dfrac{1}{6}$

(v) $r - q = 2\dfrac{4}{7} - \dfrac{1}{2} = \dfrac{18}{7} - \dfrac{1}{2} = \dfrac{36}{14} - \dfrac{7}{14} = \dfrac{29}{14} = 2\dfrac{1}{14}$

(vi) $r - s = 2\dfrac{4}{7} - 1\dfrac{1}{5} = \dfrac{18}{7} - \dfrac{6}{5} = \dfrac{90}{35} - \dfrac{42}{35} = \dfrac{48}{35} = 1\dfrac{13}{35}$

(vii) $p \times q = \dfrac{2}{3} \times \dfrac{1}{2} = \dfrac{2}{6} = \dfrac{1}{3}$

(viii) $q \times s = \dfrac{1}{2} \times 1\dfrac{1}{5} = \dfrac{1}{2} \times \dfrac{6}{5} = \dfrac{6}{10} = \dfrac{3}{5}$

(ix) $r \times s = 2\dfrac{4}{7} \times 1\dfrac{1}{5} = \dfrac{18}{7} \times \dfrac{6}{5} = \dfrac{108}{35} = 3\dfrac{3}{35}$

(x) $p \div q = \dfrac{2}{3} \div \dfrac{1}{2} = \dfrac{2}{3} \times \dfrac{2}{1} = \dfrac{4}{3} = 1\dfrac{1}{3}$

(xi) $q \div p = \dfrac{1}{2} \div \dfrac{2}{3} = \dfrac{1}{2} \times \dfrac{3}{2} = \dfrac{3}{4}$

(xii) $q \div r = \dfrac{1}{2} \div 2\dfrac{4}{7} = \dfrac{1}{2} \times \dfrac{7}{18} = \dfrac{7}{36}$

4 (i) $\dfrac{5}{8} = 0.625$

$$8 \overline{)5.^50^20^40}$$
$$\quad\; 0.\,6\,2\,5$$

(ii) $\dfrac{7}{20} = 0.35$

$$20 \overline{)7.^70^10 0}$$
$$\qquad\; 0.\,3\,5$$

(ii) $65\% = 0.65$

(iv) $0.1\% = 0.001$

5 (i) $0.375 = \dfrac{375}{1000} = \dfrac{3}{8}$

(ii) $0.28 = \dfrac{28}{100} = \dfrac{14}{50} = \dfrac{7}{25}$

(iii) $76\% = \dfrac{76}{100} = \dfrac{38}{50} = \dfrac{19}{25}$

6 (i) $\dfrac{84}{96} = \dfrac{42}{48} = \dfrac{21}{24} = \dfrac{7}{8}$

(ii) $\dfrac{84}{91} = \dfrac{12}{13}$

7 (i) $\dfrac{5}{8} = 0.625 = 62.5\%$

(ii) $0.375 = 37.5\%$

(iii) $\dfrac{7}{20} = 0.35 = 35\%$

8 4% cheaper:

Let the original price be £100.
After a 20% increase the price is £120.
In the sales the price is reduced by 20% of £120 = £24.
The price in the sales is £96.
This is an overall reduction of 4%.

9 The two prices are the same:

Let the original price be £100.
An increase of 25% gives a new price of £125.
20% of £125 is £25.
The reduced price is £100.

10 In the first game the team scored 24 points; in the second game they scored 30 points. There was an increase of 6 points from the first game to the second game. As a percentage this increase can be represented as $\dfrac{6}{24} \times 100\% = 25\%$

11 For every £5 raised Edward contributed £2 (i.e. $\dfrac{2}{5}$) and Katherine contributed £3 (i.e. $\dfrac{3}{5}$). Applying this to the £160 total raised gives:

Edward: $\dfrac{2}{5} \times £160 = £64,$

Katherine: $\dfrac{3}{5} \times £160 = £96.$

Primary pupils should have the opportunity to use ratios in appropriate contexts. The following problem is suitable for primary pupils: 'Blue and yellow paint are mixed in the proportion 3:1 to produce dark green paint. If the ratio of blue to yellow paint is 1:3 what will the resulting paint look like?'

12 This is the same type of problem as question 11, only slightly larger.

The books are shared in the ratio 52 (i.e. $\dfrac{52}{200}$) to 68 (i.e. $\dfrac{68}{200}$) to 44 (i.e. $\dfrac{44}{200}$) to 36 (i.e. $\dfrac{36}{200}$). Applying this to

Year 3: $\dfrac{52}{200} \times 1000$ books = 260 books

Year 4: $\dfrac{68}{200} \times 1000$ books = 340 books

Year 5: $\dfrac{44}{200} \times 1000$ books = 220 books

Year 6: $\dfrac{36}{200} \times 1000$ books = 180 books

13 (i) ✓ all recurring decimals are rational i.e. can be expressed as a fraction.

In this case the fraction is 36/99 = 4/11

(ii) ✗

In general, unless the number is a perfect square, the square root of an integer is irrational.

(iii) ✓

4 is a perfect square.

$\sqrt{4} = 2$.

(iv) Although there is a pattern to the sequence of numbers it is not a repeating pattern. The number is irrational. ✗

(v) ✗

π is irrational. It is non-terminating and is not a repeating decimal.

(vi) ✗

$\sqrt{8} = 2\sqrt{2}$.

It is irrational.

Any irrational number multiplied by a rational number is an irrational number.

(vii) ✗

An irrational number multiplied by a rational number is an irrational number

(viii) ✓

$\sqrt{2} \times \sqrt{8} = \sqrt{16} = 4.$

This is rational.

(ix) $\sqrt{8} + \sqrt{8} = 2\sqrt{8}.$

This is irrational.

14 First express each number as a decimal fraction correct to three decimal places:

71% = 0.710   5/7 = 0.714   18/25 = 0.720 $\sqrt{\frac{1}{2}}$ = 0.707   0.7 = 0.700

In order of size, smallest first, the numbers are: 0.7, $\sqrt{\frac{1}{2}}$, 71%, 5/7, 18/25

Give yourself 3 marks if the numbers are in the correct order. Subtract 1 mark for each number not in its correct position.

15 (i) 0.2$\dot{7}$ (ii) 0.2$\dot{7}$ (iii) 0.9$\dot{0}\dot{4}$ (iv) 18.1$\dot{8}$

Note that all rational numbers can be expressed as terminating decimals or recurring decimals.

Older primary school pupils should have the opportunity to investigate vulgar fractions and their decimal fraction equivalent. For example 1/7 expressed as a decimal fraction is 0.$\dot{1}$4285$\dot{7}$. An interesting investigation is to examine the decimal fractions of 2/7, 3/7, 4/7, 5/7, 6/7.

Similar investigations of fractions of the form 1/a, 2/a, 3/a .... where a is a prime number, reveal interesting patterns.

A difference between calculators used in the primary school and scientific calculators is that recurring decimals are truncated by a primary calculator but rounded by a scientific calculator. For example, 0.666666666... is truncated to 0.666666 on a primary calculator whereas a scientific calculator gives the answer as 0.666667.

16 (i) $100\,000 = 10^5$ (ii) $0.1 = 10^{-1}$ (iii) $100 = 10^2$

17 (i) $6.6 \times 10^3 = 6600$ (ii) $7.07 \times 10^{-2} = 0.0707$

18 (i) $523\,000 = 5.23 \times 10^5$ (ii) $0.0606 = 6.06 \times 10^{-2}$

19 (i)   ✓ Division is right distributive over addition. In other words, if the division sign is on the right-hand side of the bracket, division is distributive over addition. For example, $(300 + 30 + 3) \div 3 = 100 + 10 + 1$.

Note also that division is right distributive over subtraction. For example, $(300 - 30 - 3) \div 3 = 100 - 10 - 1.$

(ii)   ✗ Division is not left distributive over addition. In other words, if the division sign is on the left-hand side of the bracket, division is not distributive over addition. For example, $300 \div (100 + 10) \neq 3 + 30.$

(iii)   ✓ Multiplication is distributive over addition. Note that multiplication is left distributive and right distributive over addition. For example, $3 \times (100 + 10 + 1) = 300 + 30 + 3$ and $(100 + 10 + 1) \times 3 = 300 + 30 + 3.$

(iv) ✓Multiplication is distributive over subtraction. Note that multiplication is left distributive and right distributive over subtraction. For example, $5 \times (1000 - 1) = 5000 - 5$ and $(1000 - 1) \times 5 = 5000 - 5$.

Primary pupils are not expected to be familiar with the term 'distributive'. They should, however, be able to use the distributive property of multiplication to solve problems of the kind 'find the cost of five T-shirts at £9.99 each'.

(v) ✗ Division is not associative. For example, $(27 \div 9) \div 3 = 1$ whereas $27 \div (9 \div 3) = 9$. Note that it is possible to have numerous different answers to a division problem, depending on where the brackets are placed. For example, $128 \div 32 \div 8 \div 4 \div 2 \div 2$ has a number of answers, depending on where the brackets are placed. This is an interesting investigation for young children: to find out how many different answers are possible by placing brackets in different positions.

(vi) ✓Addition is associative. Even at Key Stage 1 children should be introduced to this concept. For example, $6 + 12 + 8 + 9 + 11$ is made considerably easier if $12 + 8$ and $9 + 11$ are calculated first.

(vii) ✗Subtraction is not associative. For example, $(10 - 7) - 3 = 0$ whereas $10 - (7 - 3) = 6$. As with division, it is possible to have a large number of answers to a subtraction problem, depending on where the brackets are placed. For example, $150 - 60 - 30 - 20 - 10$ has a number of answers, depending on where the brackets are placed. This is an interesting investigation for young children: to find out how many different answers are possible by placing the brackets in different positions.

(viii) ✓ Multiplication is associative. Some calculations are made significantly easier if this property of multiplication is used. For example, $17 \times 4 \times 25 \times 50 \times 2$ is simplified if it is written as $17 \times (4 \times 25) \times (50 \times 2)$.

(ix) ✓Multiplication is commutative. Primary school children need to understand this property of multiplication. Pupils need to know, for example, that 8×9 is the same as 9×8.

It is not immediately obvious to pupils (or adults) that 24% of £25 is the same as 25% of £24. It is far easier calculating 25% of £24.

(x) ✓ Multiplication is distributive over addition. Primary school children need to have experience of this kind of calculation. In primary school pupils are introduced to long multiplication by using grid multiplication.

	30	9
20	600	180
8	240	72

The diagram shows how primary school pupils are introduced to the multiplication of 28 by 39.

$28 \times 39 = 600 + 240 + 180 + 72 = 1092$.

20 (i)   Factors of 24: 1, 2, 3, 4, 6, 8, 12, 24

24 has a large number of factors. (This is one of the reasons why the Babylonians decided there should be 24 hours in a day.)

(ii)   Factors of 360: 1, 2, 3, 4, 5, 6, 8, 9, 10, 12, 15, 18, 20, 24, 30, 36, 40, 45, 60, 72, 90, 120, 180, 360

360 has a large number of factors. (This is one of the reasons why the Babylonians decided there should be 360 degrees in a full turn.)

21 (i)   49 has three factors: 1, 7, 49

(ii)   In general, all square numbers have an odd number of factors.

This is a result that primary school children should know. The following problem is a suitable investigation for primary school children. It leads to the result that all square numbers have an odd number of factors.

A prison has 100 prisoners held in 100 cells numbered 1 to 100.

This is a high security prison with 100 warders. One night the first warder went to every cell and locked it. The second warder then visited every second cell and turned the key – every second cell was now unlocked. The third warder then went to every third cell and turned the key – the third cell was now unlocked, the sixth cell was now locked, the ninth cell was unlocked. The fourth warder then went to every fourth cell and turned the key. The fourth cell was now locked. In this way each warder visited a group of cells. Which cells are locked at the end of the night?

The locked cells are numbers 1 4 9 16 25 36 49 64 81 100

Each of these cells is visited an odd number of times by a warder because square numbers have an odd number of factors.

22 (i) $48 = 2 \times 2 \times 2 \times 2 \times 3$

(ii) $105 = 3 \times 5 \times 7$

(iii) $36 = 2 \times 2 \times 3 \times 3$

(iv) $56 = 2 \times 2 \times 2 \times 7$

23 (i)   The highest common factor of 36 and 48 is $2 \times 2 \times 3 = 12$.

(ii)   The highest common factor of 105 and 56 is 7.

(iii)   The highest common factor of a^2b^2 and a^3b is a^2b.

(v)   The highest common factor of abc and cd^3 is c.

Year 6 pupils will be introduced to letters representing numbers. It is important that they view algebra as an extension of arithmetic. The highest common factor of 2^33^2 and 2^23^3 is 2^23^2. Similarly, the highest common factor of a^3b^2 and a^2b^3 is a^2b^2.

24 (i) 888

(ii) 1999

(iii) 2220

25 (i) CCCXXXIII

(ii) CDXLIV

(iii) MMXIII

26 (i) 37203

(ii) 203001050

(iii) 9000017. It is quite common for pupils to write 900000017. Teachers need to be aware of pupils' misconceptions in writing large numbers.

27 (i) Forty million four hundred and four thousand and forty

(ii) Seventy million seven thousand and seven (note that some children would interpret this number as seven thousand seven hundred and seven)

(iii) Three hundred million thirty thousand and three

Primary pupils are expected to be able to write numbers up to 10 million. The media make reference to numbers such as billion, trillion and quadrillion. A primary teacher should know what size these numbers are.

28

Primary calculator	Scientific calculator
(i) 27	13
(ii) 6	6
(iii) 5	9
(iv) 28	28
(v) 29	16
(vi) 6	8
(vii) 28	19
(viii) 4	6
(ix) 16	16
(x) 5	17

Scientific calculators are programmed to carry out calculations in the order Brackets, Index, Division, Multiplication, Addition, Subtraction. The acronym BIDMAS is often used to describe this.

For example, $2 + 3^2 + (8 + 4) \div 3 = 2 + 3^2 + 12 \div 3 = 2 + 9 + 12 \div 3 = 2 + 9 + 4 = 15$.

29 (i)   7. In binary notation the right-hand column is the units column, the next column the 2s column, the next column the 4s and so on in multiples of 2. 1 +2 + 4 = 7.

(ii)   14. 2 + 4 + 8 = 14. Note that adding a zero to a number in binary notation multiplies the number by 2.

30 (i)   16 + 8 = 24 and hence 11000 is the binary representation of 24.

(ii)   32 + 16 = 48 and hence 110000 is the binary representation of 48.

Pupils should understand what a binary number is and why it is important in the context of computing.

Algebra – Patterns and relationships

1 (i) $ab = 5 \times 15 = 75$

(ii) $ac = 5 \times 2 = 10$

(iii) $de = 15$ and $d = 3$, hence $e = 15 \div 3 = 5$

(iv) $df = 18$ and $d = 3$, hence $f = 18 \div 3 = 6$

(v) $a(b + c) = 5(15 + 2) = 85$

(vi) $d(e + f) = 3(5 + 6) = 33$

(vii) $a(b - c) = 5(15 - 2) = 65$

(viii) $d(e - f) = 3(5 - 6) = -3$

(ix) $2a^2b = 2 \times 5^2 \times 15 = 750$

(x) $2d^2e = 2 \times 3^2 \times 5 = 90$

(xi) $\dfrac{1}{a} = \dfrac{1}{5}$ or 0.2

(xii) $\dfrac{1}{d} = \dfrac{1}{3}$ or 0.333

2 (i)   36

(ii)   100

(iii) n^2

3 (i)   8, 12, 16, 20, 24

(ii)   44 slabs

(iii) $4n + 4$ or alternatively $4(n + 1)$

4 (i)   64

(ii)   512

(iii) $2(n - 1)$

5 (i)   1, 3, 6, 10, 15

(ii)   55 cubes

(iii) $\dfrac{n(n + 1)}{2}$

Examples of triangle numbers in different contexts should be given to pupils. For example, pharmacists when counting circular tablets use a triangular scoop that is calibrated in triangular numbers. The numbers on the side of the scoop are 1, 3, 6, 10,..., showing how many tablets are in the triangular scoop.

6 (i) $\dfrac{1}{x+2} = 3$ 　　　　(ii) $\dfrac{1}{5x-4} = \dfrac{1}{x}$

　　　　$1 = 3(x+2)$ 　　　　　　　$x = 5x - 4$

　　　　$1 = 3x+6$ 　　　　　　　$4 = 4x$

　　　　$-5 = 3x$ 　　　　　　　$x = 1$

　　　　$x = -\dfrac{5}{3}$

(iii) $\dfrac{3}{1+b} = \dfrac{5}{b+3}$

　　　$3(b + 3) = 5(1 + b)$

　　　$3b + 9 = 5 + 5b$

　　　　$4 = 2b$

　　　　$2 = b$

7 (i) $\begin{cases} y - 2x = 4 & (1) \\ y + x = 7 & (2) \end{cases}$

$(2) - (1)$:

$$\begin{array}{r} y + x = 7 \\ y - 2x = 4 \\ \hline 3x = 3 \\ x = 1 \end{array}$$

Substitute in (2):

　　　$y + x = 7$

　　　$y + 1 = 7$

　　　　$y = 6$

(ii) $\begin{cases} 2x - 3y = 2 & (1) \\ 4x + 6y = 4 & (2) \end{cases}$

Rearranging (1) gives:

$$x = \dfrac{2+3y}{2}$$

Substituting for x in (2) gives:

　　　$4x + 6y = 4$

　　$4\left(\dfrac{2+3y}{2}\right) + 6y = 4$

$4 + 6y + 6y = 4$

$12y = 0$

$y = 0$

Substituting for y in (1) gives:

$2x - 3y = 2$

$2x - 0 = 2$

$x = 1$

(iii) $\begin{cases} 2x - y = 5 \\ 3x + 2y = 11 \end{cases}$

By drawing the graphs represented by the two equations it is possible to find the common solution. The common solution is found where the two lines cross. At this point the values for x and y in both of the equations are the same.

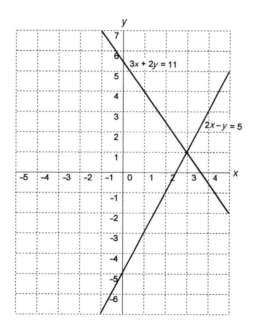

In this case the lines cross at the point (3,1), giving the common solution $x = 3$ and $y = 1$.

8 (i) There are no real solutions. Any real number when squared gives a positive answer. For example $-2 \times -2 = 4$. Only imaginary numbers when squared give a negative answer!

(ii) There is an infinite number of solutions of this equation. In fact any number would satisfy this equation.

(iii) $x = 2$ is the unique solution of this equation

9 (i)   True

   (ii)   False. If $x < -4$ then $x^2 > 16$.

   (iii) True

   (iv) True

   (v)   True

   (vi) True

   (vii) False. If $6 - x > 10$ then $x < -4$.

Shape and space

1 $b = 80°, c = 100°, d = 80°, e = 100°, f = 100°$.

Opposite angles are equal. Complementary angles sum to 90°. Supplementary angles sum to 180°.

2 Angle $d = 80°$.

3

6 lines of reflective symmetry
rotational symmetry of order 6

no lines of reflective symmetry
rotational symmetry of order 2

1 line of reflective symmetry
rotational symmetry of order 1

4 lines of reflective symmetry
rotational symmetry of order 4

2 lines of reflective symmetry
rotational symmetry of order 2

Primary pupils are encouraged to examine the properties of shapes by considering their order of rotational symmetry and the number of lines of symmetry. For example, quadrilaterals can be categorised by their symmetry properties.

	Number of lines of symmetry passing through corners	Number of lines of symmetry passing through the mid-points of sides	Order of rotational symmetry
Square	2	2	4
Rectangle		2	2 (at least)
Rhombus	2		2 (at least)

	Number of lines of symmetry passing through corners	Number of lines of symmetry passing through the mid-points of sides	Order of rotational symmetry
Parallelogram			2 (at least)
Kite	1 (at least)		
Isosceles trapezium		1 (at least)	

See Mooney et al., *Primary Mathematics: Knowledge and Understanding*, for further explanation.

4 angle a: right   angle b: reflex   angle c: acute   angle d: reflex

angle e: acute   angle f: right   angle g: obtuse

An acute angle is one that is less than 90 degrees.

An obtuse angle is between 90 and 180 degrees.

A reflex angle is between 180 and 360 degrees.

5 (i)   Shapes A and B are congruent. Two shapes are congruent if the angles are the same and the lengths are the same.

(ii)   All of the other shapes, A, B and D are similar to shape C. Shapes are similar if their angles are the same and the ratio of the lengths of sides is the same.

6 A regular triangle is called an *equilateral* triangle. Because it is a regular polygon it is clear that all the sides are of *equal length* and all the angles are the same size, i.e. *60°*.

Again because an *equilateral* triangle is regular it has *three* lines of reflective symmetry and rotational symmetry of order *3*.

A triangle which has two sides of equal length is called an *isosceles* triangle. As well as having two sides of equal length an *isosceles* triangle also has *two* angles of equal size. An *isosceles* triangle has *one* line of reflective symmetry and rotational symmetry of order *1*.

A triangle which has three sides of different length and no equal angles is called a *scalene* triangle. *Scalene* triangles have *no* lines of reflective symmetry and rotational symmetry of order *1*. (Note that all shapes have a rotational symmetry of at least 1.)

A triangle containing one angle of 90° is called a *right-angled* triangle. A *right-angled* triangle must be either an *isosceles* or *scalene* triangle. A right-angled triangle cannot be *equilateral*.

The number of lines of reflective symmetry of a *right-angled* triangle depends on whether it is an *isosceles* or *scalene* triangle.

A triangle with an obtuse angle cannot be *right-angled*.

7 Right-angled triangles satisfy Pythagoras' theorem, i.e. $a^2 + b^2 = c^2$.

    (i) $3^2 + 4^2 = 5^2$, hence the triangle has a right angle. Any triangle whose lengths of sides are multiples of 3, 4 and 5 will be a right-angled triangle. For example a triangle with sides 6, 8 and 10 will have a right angle.

        There is an infinite number of right-angled triangles. For example, a triangle with sides 8, 15 and 17 is right-angled. Year 6 pupils should be encouraged to find other right-angled triangles.

    (ii) $4^2 + 5^2 = 41 \neq 6^2$, hence the triangle does not have a right angle.

8 Area of the triangle is equal to half $\times$ base $\times$ height $= 2$ cm $\times$ 3 cm $= 6$cm^2.

9 Area of the parallelogram is equal to base $\times$ height $= 8$ cm $\times$ 5 cm $= 40$ cm^2.

10 The area of the trapezium is found by dissecting it into a parallelogram and a triangle, then adding the area of the parallelogram and the area of the triangle:

Area of parallelogram + Area of triangle = (5 cm $\times$ 4 cm) + (1.5 cm $\times$ 4 cm)

$$= 20 \text{ cm}^2 + 6 \text{ cm}^2$$

$$= 26 \text{ cm}^2$$

11 Perimeter $= 7$ cm $+ 3$ cm$+3$ cm$+6$ cm $+ (7 - 3)$ cm$+ (6 - 3)$ cm

$$= 7 \text{ cm} +3 \text{ cm} +3 \text{ cm} +6 \text{ cm} +4 \text{ cm} +3 \text{ cm}$$

$$= 26 \text{ cm}$$

Area $= (7 \times 6)$ cm$^2 - (4 \times 3)$ cm^2

$$= 42 \text{ cm}^2 - 12 \text{ cm}^2$$

$$= 30 \text{ cm}^2$$

12 Using Pythagoras' theorem to calculate L:

$4^2 + 5^2 = L^2$

$16 + 25 = L^2$

$41 = L^2$

$\sqrt{41} = L$

$L \approx 6.4$ cm

Perimeter ≈ 2 cm $+ 13$ cm $+ 8$ cm $+ 5$ cm $+ 6$ cm $+ 3$ cm $+ 4$ cm $+ 6.4$ cm

$$\approx 47.4 \text{ cm}$$

Area $= (2 \times 13)$ cm$^2 + (6 \times 5)$ cm$^2 + (\frac{1}{2} \times 4 \times 5)$ cm^2

$$= 26 \text{ cm}^2 + 30 \text{ cm}^2 + 10 \text{ cm}^2$$

$$= 66 \text{ cm}^2$$

Pupils should investigate rectangles that have the same perimeter but different areas. It is a common misconception to think that if two shapes have the same perimeter they have the same area.

13 Circumference = πd

$$= 10\pi \text{ cm}$$

$$\approx 31.4 \text{ cm (taking } \pi \text{ to be 3.14)}$$

Area = πr^2

$$= 25\pi \text{ cm}^2$$

$$\approx 78.5 \text{ cm}^2 \text{ (taking } \pi \text{ to be 3.14)}$$

Pupils should be encouraged to investigate the circumference of everyday objects. For example, to investigate how far a bicycle moves when the wheels rotate once.

14 (i) Area of circle A = πr^2

$$= 25 \pi \text{ cm}^2$$

$$\approx 78.5 \text{ cm}^2$$

The sector marked in circle A represents $\frac{1}{3}$ of the circle because 120° is $\frac{1}{3}$ of 360°. Hence the area of the sector in circle A is $\frac{1}{3} \times 78.5 \text{ cm}^2 \approx 26.2 \text{ cm}^2$

Area of circle B = πr^2

$$= 9\pi \text{ cm}^2$$

$$\approx 28.3 \text{ cm}^2$$

The sector marked in circle B represents $\frac{1}{8}$ of the circle because 45° is $\frac{1}{8}$ of 360°.

Hence the area of the sector in circle B is $\frac{1}{8} \times 28.3 \text{ cm}^2 \approx 3.5 \text{ cm}^2$

(ii) The circumference of circle A = $2\pi r$

$$= 10\pi \text{ cm}$$

$$\approx 31.4 \text{ cm}$$

The length of the arc marked in circle A represents $\frac{1}{3}$ of the length of the circumference because 120° is $\frac{1}{3}$ of 360°. Hence the length of the arc in circle A is $\frac{1}{3} \times 31.4 \text{ cm} \approx 10.5 \text{ cm}$.

The circumference of circle B = $2\pi r$

$$= 6\pi \text{ cm}$$

$$\approx 18.8 \text{ cm}$$

The length of the arc marked in circle B represents $\frac{1}{8}$ the length of the circumference because 45° is $\frac{1}{8}$ of 360°. Hence the length of the arc in circle B is $\frac{1}{8} \times 18.8 \text{ cm} \approx 2.4 \text{ cm}$

Older pupils should be encouraged to use this approach to calculate the distance from, say, Ecuador to Kenya along the equator.

15 (i)   Reflection in the y-axis has the effect of multiplying the x-coordinate (or abscissa) by –1, giving:

$a' = (-1, 1)$
$b' = (-1, 3)$
$c' = (-5, 3)$
$d' = (-5, 1)$

(ii)   The new coordinates are

$a'' = (1, -1)$
$b'' = (3, -1)$
$c'' = (3, -5)$
$d'' = (1, -5)$

Do you notice a pattern in the new coordinates?

Older primary pupils are expected to be able to plot points in each of the four quadrants. They should be encouraged to investigate problems such as 'Rotate the rectangle with coordinates (0,0) (2,0) (2,3) (0,3) 180 degrees about the point (0,0). What do you notice about the new coordinates?'

16 The five Platonic solids are:

- regular tetrahedron (this solid is made up of four regular triangles);
- cube (regular hexahedron) (this solid is made up of six regular quadrilaterals);
- regular octahedron (this solid is made up eight regular triangles);
- regular dodecahedron (this solid is made up of 12 regular pentagons);
- regular icosahedron (this solid is made up of 20 regular triangles).

The Platonic solids are the only regular solids. A polyhedron is defined as regular if all its faces are identical and regular and the same number of faces meet at each vertex.

(There are some solids whose faces are all regular but not identical. For example, a polyhedron with four regular triangles and four regular hexagons is called an Archimedean solid.

There are some solids whose faces are all regular and identical but the number of faces meeting at a vertex is not constant. For example, a bi-pyramid consists of six equilateral triangles. The number of triangles meeting at a vertex is 3 or 4.

A solid may have faces all of the same type and not be a Platonic solid. For example, a polyhedron with six faces which are parallelograms is called a parallelepiped.)

17

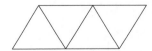
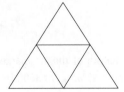

18

19

Solid	Faces	Edges	Vertices
Cube	6	12	8
Tetrahedron	4	6	4
Triangular prism	5	9	6

Euler's law states that the number of faces of a polyhedron plus the number of vertices minus two equals the number of edges. Older primary school pupils should be familiar with this law. Older pupils should have the opportunity to discover relations between the number of faces, vertices and edges of a polyhedron. For example, pupils should have the opportunity to discover that if a polyhedron is a pyramid the number of vertices is the same as the number of faces.

20 (i) The cuboid has:

2 faces with an area of 3 cm × 4 cm = 12 cm^2
2 faces with an area of 4 cm × 6 cm = 24 cm^2
2 faces with an area of 3 cm × 6 cm = 18 cm^2

(ii) The total surface area = (2 × 12 cm^2) + (2 × 24 cm^2) + (2 × 18 cm^2)
= 24 cm^2 + 48 cm^2 + 36 cm^2
= 108 cm^2

(iii) The volume of the cuboid = 3cm × 4 cm × 6 cm
= 72 cm^3

21 Surface area:

Area of each circular face $= \pi r^2$

$= 25\pi$ cm^2

≈ 78.5 cm^2

Area of curved surface $= 10 \times 2\pi r$ cm^2

$= 10 \times 10\pi$ cm^2

≈ 314 cm^2

Total surface area $= (2 \times 25\pi$ cm$^2) + 100\pi$ cm^2

≈ 157 cm$^2 + 314$ cm^2

$= 471$ cm^2

Volume:

Area of circular face $\times$ length $= 78.5$ cm$^2 \times 10$ cm

$= 785$ cm^3

Pupils should be encouraged to investigate the dimensions of labels on cans and discover the relation between the width of the label and the diameter of the can.

22 Surface area:

Area of each triangular face $= 6$ cm $\times 8$ cm

$= 48$ cm^2

Area of 2 rectangular faces $= 10$ cm $\times 20$ cm

$= 200$ cm^2

Area of remaining rectangular face $= 12$ cm $\times 20$ cm

$= 240$ cm^2

Total surface area $= (2 \times 48$ cm$^2) + (2 \times 200$ cm$^2) + 240$ cm^2

$= 96$ cm$^2 + 400$ cm$^2 + 240$ cm^2

$= 736$ cm^2

Volume:

Area of triangular face $\times$ length $= 48$ cm$^2 \times 20$ cm

$= 960$ cm^3

Using Pythagoras $10^2 = 6^2 + h^2$

$10^2 - 6^2 = h^2$

$100 - 36 = h^2$

$64 = h^2$

$h = 8$ cm

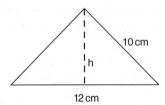

Pupils should be encouraged to construct cuboids from card of a fixed size – say, card of area 500 cm^2 – and try to find the largest volume they can enclose.

23 (i) False. A prism has the same cross-section throughout its length. A cuboid, for example, is a prism. An octahedron is not a prism.

(ii) True. It is possible for the polyhedron not to be a pyramid. A compound shape consisting of a square-based pyramid on top of a cube has 9 faces, 9 vertices and 16 edges. A pyramid with an octagonal base also has 9 faces, 9 vertices and 16 edges.

(iii) True. A cuboid is a prism. It has a cross section that is a rectangle.

(iv) False. A dodecahedron has 12 faces, 20 vertices and 30 edges.

(v) True. An icosahedron has 20 faces, 12 vertices and 30 edges. The icosahedron is the dual of the dodecahedron.

(vi) True. An octahedron has 8 faces, 6 vertices and 12 edges.

(vii) True. A cube has 6 faces, 8 vertices and 12 edges. The cube is the dual of the octahedron.

(viii) True. A pyramid with a hexagonal base has 7 faces, 7 vertices and 12 edges.

(ix) False. A tetrahedron has 6 planes of symmetry. A tetrahedron has 6 edges. The planes of symmetry pass through an edge and the opposite face.

(x) True. A triangular prism has 5 faces.

Pupils should be encouraged to assemble and disassemble polyhedra.

There are numerous appropriate 3-D investigations and problems that pupils can attempt. For example, 'Alisha says she has made a 3-D shape with 7 vertices, 6 faces and 11 edges. Do you think she is right?'

Statistics

1 Mode = 3 Median = 3 Mean = 4

2 Size 8 is the mode. The mode is sometimes called the shopkeeper's average. Shopkeepers use an average that represents the most popular product.

£21500 is the median. The median is not affected by very large values, whereas the mean is. For this reason the government uses the median to represent the country's average wage.

80 kg is the mean. The total weight in the lift is crucial. The mean allows the total weight to be calculated.

Pupils are expected to know how to find the different averages but also, equally important, to understand the contexts in which they are used.

3 Lower quartile = 3
Median = 6
Upper quartile = 9
Range = 9
Inter-quartile range = 6

4 (i) Alf. He scored 400 runs.

(ii) Bill is the most consistent.

(iii) Alf

(iv) Alf

5 Modes = 2 and 5. There are two modes. This is an example of a bimodal distribution.

Median = 4.5. The median is midway between the two middle values. If there is an even number of values it is possible the median is not a member of the data set.

Mean = 4

6 (i) 21

(ii) 6

(iii) One pupil has a reading age of 7 years 7 months and a chronological age of 6 years 1 month.

A scatter diagram is used for bivariate data. For example, pupils' height and shoe size could be plotted on a scatter diagram. The relationship between height and shoe size is immediately apparent when displayed in this way. Older primary pupils should be able to use and interpret scatter diagrams.

7 (i) 30

(ii) 20

(iii) 24

(iv) Test 2

8 (i) False. There are 182 pupils. 3/7 of 182 is 78.

(ii) True

(iii) False. 2/7 of 182 is 52.

9 (i) 50

(ii) 40 degrees Celsius

(iii) 100

Pupils should be able to use conversion graphs to convert, for example, pounds (sterling) to euros, pounds (mass) to kilograms, gallons to litres.

10 (i) Categoric. Eye colour is not a quantitative variable. A variable that is not quantitative is called categoric or qualitative.

(ii) Discrete. Shoe size is a quantitative variable. However, it only takes particular values. Other examples of discrete variables are: number of siblings, dress size.

(iii) Categoric (or qualitative)

    (iv)   Continuous. The height of something is measured on a continuous scale.

    (v)   Continuous. The weight of something is measured on a continuous scale.

In Key Stage 1 pupils, for the most part, investigate categoric data. The average they find is the mode and the appropriate diagram to represent the data is usually a block graph or a bar chart.

In Key Stage 2 pupils investigate discrete and continuous data. They calculate the median and the mean and use a variety of diagrams to represent their data.

Probability

1 (i) $\dfrac{1}{36}$ (ii) $\dfrac{6}{36} = \dfrac{1}{6}$ (iii) $\dfrac{5}{36}$ (iv)   0

2 (i) $\dfrac{1}{6}$ (ii) $\dfrac{1}{2}$ (iii) $\dfrac{1}{6} \times \dfrac{1}{2} = \dfrac{1}{12}$

3 (i) $\dfrac{13}{52} = \dfrac{1}{4}$ (ii) $\dfrac{26}{52} = \dfrac{1}{2}$ (iii) $\dfrac{32}{52} = \dfrac{16}{26} = \dfrac{8}{13}$ (iv) $\dfrac{12}{52} = \dfrac{6}{26} = \dfrac{3}{13}$

    (iii) and (iv) can be answered by thinking in terms of each suit rather than the whole pack of cards. In each suit of 13 there are 8 cards less than a 10, and 3 higher than a Jack.

4 (i)   12/51 = 4/17   (ii)   36/51 = 12/17   (iii)   3/51 = 1/17

5 (i)   An 8 is the worst card. It is the middle card. If the contestant has an 8 and guesses higher there is a 24/51 (= 8/17) chance of being correct.

    (ii)   Ace and 2 are the best cards. If the contestant has an Ace and guesses the next card will be lower there is a 48/51 (= 16/17) chance of being correct.

6 (i)   He is not correct. There is an equal number of even and odd cards, therefore it is equally likely that he will have an even number or an odd number.

    (ii)   (a) unlikely

          (b) certain

7 (i)   False. There are four equally likely outcomes, HH HT TH TT. The probability of two heads is 1/4.

    (ii)   True. If the total is 12 then each dice must show a 6. The probability both dice show a 6 is 1/6 × 1/6 = 1/36. The two events are independent of each other.

    (iii)   False. The probability the first card is a heart is 13/52 (= 1/4). The probability the second card is a heart is 12/51 (= 4/17). The probability both cards are hearts is 1/4 × 4/17 = 1/17. And 1/17 < 1/16. The two events are not independent of each other.

    (iv)   True. The probability the first card is black is 26/52 (=1/2). The probability the second card is black is 25/51. The probability both cards are black is 1/2 × 25/51 = 25/102. And 25/102 <1/4. The two events are not independent of each other.

(v)   True. If the total is 8 each dice must have 4 on its lower face. The probability 4 is underneath on the first dice is 1/4. The probability 4 is underneath on the second dice is 1/4. The probability of having two fours is 1/4 × 1/4 = 1/16. The two events are independent of each other.

It is a common mistake to confuse dependent and independent events. A recent article in a newspaper reported that a woman had had two sets on non-identical twins and that the probability of this happening was 1/85 × 1/85. The probability of someone having non-identical twins is 1/85. The probability of someone having two sets of non-identical twins, however, is not 1/85 × 1/85. If someone has had one set of non-identical twins the probability of having another set is greater than 1/85. The events are not independent. The probability of having two sets of non-identical twins is greater than 1/85 × 1/85.

Measures

1 (i)   yard   metre

(ii)   pound   kilogram

(iii)   mile   kilometre

(iv)   square inch   square centimetre

(v)   acre   hectare

(vi)   ounce   gram

(vii)   pint   litre

(viii) ton   tonne

There is very little difference between a ton and a tonne. A ton is 2240 pounds and a tonne is 1000 kg.

(ix)   miles per hour   kilometres per hour

(x)   inches per minute   centimetres per minute

(xi)   inches per year   centimetres per year

(xii)   cubic inches   cubic centimetres

2 (i)   Hectare. A hectare is 10000 square metres. An acre is 4840 square yards. A hectare is more than twice the size of an acre. Historically an acre was defined as a rectangular field that was a furlong (= 220 yards) long and a chain (= 22 yards) wide.

(ii)   2 pints. A litre is approximately $1\frac{3}{4}$ pints.

(iii)   Kilogram. A kilogram is approximately 2.2 pounds.

(iv)   Metre. A metre is approximately 10% more than a yard.

(v)   2 kilometres. A kilometre is approximately 5/8 mile. A kilometre is defined as 1/10000 the distance from the North Pole to the Equator.

(vi) Gallon. A gallon is 8 pints.

(vii) Inch. An inch is approximately 2.5 centimetres.

(viii) 1 kilometre. There are 8 furlongs in a mile. A furlong was considered to be the longest distance a horse could plough a straight furrow. Furrow long was abbreviated to furlong.

Although metric measures have been used in the United Kingdom for some time, Imperial measures continue to be used. Primary pupils are expected to be familiar with the common Imperial measures.

3 (i) 500 metres

(ii) 50 metres

4 (i) 10 centimetres

(ii) 1 millimetre

5 (i) 1:10000

(ii) 1:10000

(iii) 1:100000

6 (i) 36 km/hr

(ii) 6 km/hr

(iii) 1.8 km/hr

A compound measure is one with more than one unit. For example, pressure is measured in composite units, pounds per square inch. Primary pupils should have experience of using compound measures. They should be familiar, for example, with compound measures such as miles per gallon. They should be encouraged to investigate the relation between miles per gallon and gallons per 1000 miles. In the UK miles per gallon is the compound measure used, whereas in the United States gallons per 1000 miles is used and in Continental Europe litres per 100 km. It is a useful exercise to discuss the advantages and disadvantages of the different compound measures.

7 Force and weight. Weight is the force of gravity on a body. In the primary school the distinction is not usually made between mass and weight. Teachers, however, need to be aware of the difference. Bathroom scales measure weight and as such should be calibrated in newtons. If the same person used bathroom scales on the Moon the weight registered would be significantly less. Balance scales, however, measure mass. If balance scales were used on the Moon the reading would be the same.

8 10^6 bits per second

9 (i) 148 days

(ii) 181 days

10 (i)   31 leap years. Note that 1900 was not a leap year. In general, a year is a leap year if it is divisible by 4. If the year ends in 00, however, it is only a leap year if it is divisible by 400. For example, 2100 will not be a leap year. There are a little less than 365¼ days in a year. For this reason leap years occur less frequently than once every 4 years.

11 (i)   5 hours 46 minutes

(ii)   11 hours 13 minutes

12 (i)   False. The United Kingdom measure of shoe size is an interval measure. The difference in length of a size 8 shoe and a size 6 shoe is the same as the difference in length between a size 6 shoe and a size 4 shoe. The ratio of the lengths of a size 8 shoe and a size 4 shoe is not 2:1.

(ii)   False. Oven settings are measured on an interval scale. The difference in temperature between an oven setting of 8 and an oven setting of 6 is the same as the difference in temperature between an oven setting of 6 and an oven setting of 4. The ratio of the temperature of a setting of 8 to the temperature of a setting of 4 is not 2:1.

(iii)   True. Continental shoe size is measured on a ratio scale. The ratio of the lengths is 2:1.

(iv)   False. The Beaufort scale is not a ratio scale. The actual relation between the Beaufort reading, B, and the wind speed, v, is

$v = 0.836\, B^{3/2}$ m/s

If the wind speed increases by a factor of 8 the Beaufort reading increases by a factor of 4.

(v)   False. The Richter scale is not a ratio scale. An earthquake of magnitude 8 is ten times as powerful as one of magnitude 7. An earthquake of magnitude 8 is 10000 times as powerful as one of magnitude 4. The Richter scale is a geometric scale.

(vi)   False. Temperature is measured on an interval scale. But note that thermodynamic temperature is measured on a ratio scale (kelvin).

(vii)   True. Electric current is measured on a ratio scale.

(viii)   True. Speed is measured on a ratio scale.

(ix)   True. Weight is measured on a ratio scale.

(x)   False. A2 paper is twice the size of A3. A3 paper is twice the size of A4. An A2 piece of paper is four times the size of an A4 piece of paper. Paper size is measured on a geometric scale.

Pupils should be encouraged to investigate how paper is measured.

Equations and graphs

1 (i)   BC

(ii)   CD and EF

(iii)   I

(iv)   GH

(v)   Same speed. The slope of the graph indicates the speed. If the slope is positive the person is cycling away from home. If the slope is negative the person is travelling towards home.

(vi)   DE

(vii) AB

(viii) False

2 Using $y = mx + c$ as the general equation of a straight line, where m is the gradient and c is the y-intercept gives:

(i)   gradient = 10

(ii) y-intercept = 8

3 Using $y = mx + c$

m = gradient $c = y$-intercept

$\quad = \dfrac{3}{2}$ $= -2$

Substituting into the general equation gives:

$y = \dfrac{3}{2}x - 2$

4 (i)   gradient = $\dfrac{2}{3}$ y-intercept = 6

(ii)   gradient = $\dfrac{3}{2}$ y-intercept = –3

Pupils should be encouraged to investigate gradient in different contexts. For example, they should know that a hill of gradient 1 in 4 is steeper than a hill of gradient 1 in 8. In addition, they should know that the hill is twice as steep.

5 (i), (iii), (v) and (vi) are equivalent.

6 (i)   This is equivalent to $y = 10 - x$. This is the equation of a straight-line graph with gradient –1 and intercept 10.

(ii)   This is equivalent to $y = 10/x$. It is not the equation of a straight-line graph.

(iii) This is equivalent to $y = x - 10$. This is the equation of a straight-line graph with gradient 1 and intercept –10.

(iv)   This is equivalent to $y = x/10$. This is the equation of a straight-line graph with gradient 1/10 and intercept 0.

(v)   This is equivalent to $y = 4 - 2x/3$. This is the equation of a straight-line graph with gradient –2/3 and intercept 4.

(vi)   This is the equation of a straight-line graph with gradient –1 and intercept 6.

(vii)   This is not the equation of a straight-line graph.

(viii) This is not the equation of a straight-line graph.

(ix)   This is the equation of a straight-line graph with gradient ¼ and intercept 0.

(x)   This is equivalent to $y = 4/x$. This is not the equation of a straight-line graph.

Reasoning and proof

1 (i)   True. The product of an odd number and an even number always gives an even number. As one of the two numbers is even, it has a factor of 2; hence the product will have a factor of 2. This is an example of a deductive proof.

(ii)   False. This can be shown using disproof by counter-example. Let the three consecutive numbers be 2, 3, 4. Summing gives $2 + 3 + 4 = 9$. This is not even, hence the statement is false.

(iii) True. The product of three consecutive numbers is always divisible by 6. Within any three consecutive numbers one must be even and therefore have a factor of 2, and one must have a factor of 3. Hence the product will have a factor of 2×3, i.e. 6. This is an example of a deductive proof.

(iv)   True. Four consecutive numbers can be written as $x, x + 1, x + 2, x + 3$. The sum is $4x + 6 = 2(2x + 3)$. This has a factor of 2 and hence is even. This is an example of a deductive proof.

(v)   False. Consider two odd numbers, for example, 9 and 7. Subtracting gives $9 - 7 = 2$. This is an even number. This counter-example proves that the statement is false.

(vi)   True. An odd number can be written as $2x + 1$ where x is an integer. Another odd number can be written as $2y + 1$ where y is an integer. The product is $(2x + 1)(2y + 1)$ $= 4xy + 2x + 2y + 1 = 2(2xy + x + y) + 1$. This is in the form $2N + 1$ and hence is an odd number. In general, the product of two odd numbers is an odd number. This is an example of a deductive proof.

(vii) True. As in (iv), the sum of four consecutive numbers can be written as $4x + 6 = 2(2x + 3)$. $2x + 3$ is an odd number and hence $2(2x + 3)$ has a factor of 2 but not a factor of 4. This is an example of a deductive proof.

(viii) The sum of five consecutive numbers can be written as $x + x + 1 + x + 2 + x + 3 + x + 4$ $= 5x + 10 = 5(x + 2)$.

This number has a factor of 5. This is an example of a deductive proof.

Older primary pupils should understand disproof by counter-example and simple deductive proofs.

Primary pupils are not expected to be able to carry out deductive proofs using algebra. They should, however, be able to demonstrate that the sum of an odd number and an even number is an odd number. By representing an even number and an odd number using multilink it can be easily shown that the sum is odd. It is an interesting exercise for older primary pupils to demonstrate, using multilink, that the sum of five consecutive numbers is divisible by 5.

See Mooney et al., *Primary Mathematics: Knowledge and Understanding* for appropriate ways to teach proof to primary pupils.

2 (i) True (ii) False (iii) False

3 Consider the factors of all the numbers from 10 to 20:

10 has factors 1, 2, 5, 10
11 has factors 1, 11
12 has factors 1, 2, 3, 4, 6, 12
13 has factors 1, 13
14 has factors 1, 2, 7, 14
15 has factors 1, 3, 5, 15
16 has factors 1, 2, 4, 8, 16
17 has factors 1, 17
18 has factors 1, 2, 3, 6, 9, 18
19 has factors 1, 19
20 has factors 1, 2, 4, 5, 10, 20

This method of proof by exhaustion shows that there are exactly four prime numbers between 10 and 20: 11, 13, 17, 19.

4 Let the two odd numbers be $2a + 1$ and $2b + 1$ (where a and b are both integers).

Adding gives $(2a + 1) + (2b + 1) = 2a + 2b + 2 = 2(a + b + 1)$.

$a + b + 1$ is an integer, which implies that $2(a + b + 1)$ is even.

Note that it is far easier to demonstrate this result by using multilink!

5 A table can be used to show all the possible outcomes:

Die 1	Die 2	Total	Die 1	Die 2	Total	Die 1	Die 2	Total	Die 1	Die 2	Total	Die 1	Die 2	Total	Die 1	Die 2	Total
1	1	2	2	1	3	3	1	4	4	1	5	5	1	6	6	1	7
1	2	3	2	2	4	3	2	5	4	2	6	5	2	7	6	2	8
1	3	4	2	3	5	3	3	6	4	3	7	5	3	8	6	3	9
1	4	5	2	4	6	3	4	7	4	4	8	5	4	9	6	4	10
1	5	6	2	5	7	3	5	8	4	5	9	5	5	10	6	5	11
1	6	7	2	6	8	3	6	9	4	6	10	5	6	11	6	6	12

From the table it can be seen that when throwing two dice the probability of obtaining a 6 is $\frac{5}{36}$ and the probability of obtaining a 4 is $\frac{3}{36}$, which shows that 6 is a more likely outcome than 4.

An interesting activity for older primary pupils is to play bingo using two six-faced dice. Pupils draw a 3×3 grid and place numbers of their choice, between 2 and 12, in the nine squares. Note that pupils are allowed to repeat numbers. The teacher rolls the two dice and calls out the sum. The pupil crosses out that number (he or she only crosses out one number at a time), and the first pupil to cross out all nine numbers calls 'Bingo'. The 'best' bingo card will have more than one 7 and no 2 or 12. It is an interesting activity to investigate what constitutes a good card. A variation on this game is for the teacher to call out the difference between the two numbers. In this case the pupils place numbers between 0 and 5, inclusive, on their card. It is not immediately obvious what constitutes a good card.

6   The sum of any two consecutive triangle numbers is a square number.

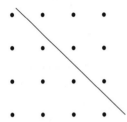

The diagram shows how two triangle numbers combine to give a square number.

There are various problems that give rise to triangle numbers. Primary pupils should be given the opportunity to investigate contexts that are of interest to them. An appropriate problem for primary pupils is: 'Twenty strangers meet and all shake hands with each other. How many handshakes are there?' This kind of problem can be tackled in a practical, logical way by considering the number of handshakes when there are 2 people, 3 people, 4 people etc. and finding the pattern.

Pupils should be encouraged to use multilink to investigate the relationship between triangle numbers and square numbers. For older primary pupils there are more interesting relationships that can be investigated, for example, 8 × any triangle number + 1 is always a square number.

7   The difference between consecutive square numbers are increasing odd numbers.

4	**4**	**4**	**4**
3	**3**	**3**	**4**
2	**2**	**3**	**4**
1	**2**	**3**	**4**

The diagram shows why the differences between consecutive square numbers are odd numbers. Pupils should be encouraged to use multilink to investigate this relationship.

8   (i)   True. A rectangle is a quadrilateral with four right angles. All squares have four right angles and hence all squares are rectangles.

(ii)   True. A rectangle is a quadrilateral with four right angles. A rhombus is a quadrilateral with all sides the same length. If a shape is a rectangle and a rhombus then it has four right angles and four sides the same length. It is therefore a square.

(iii) True. A parallelogram is a quadrilateral with its opposite angles equal. The opposite angles of a rectangle are equal. A rectangle is therefore a parallelogram.

(iv)   False. The sides of a parallelogram are not necessarily equal. A rhombus has all sides the same length. A parallelogram is therefore not necessarily a rhombus.

The curriculum encourages primary pupils to be familiar with the properties of the quadrilaterals. The quadrilaterals can, for example, be defined by the properties of their diagonals. Pupils should be encouraged to discover these properties.

	Diagonals same length	Diagonals bisect each other	Diagonals meet at right angles
Square	YES	YES	YES
Rhombus		YES	YES
Rectangle	YES	YES	
Parallelogram		YES	
Kite			YES
Isosceles trapezium	YES		

Part 6: Targets for further development

Teachers are constantly engaged in target setting, for example when assessing and marking children's work, when keeping records and when evaluating their own performance. Target setting is seen as a positive step towards ensuring progress and raising attainment. As your own training gets under way, you might well be asked to set targets for yourself. Targets will almost certainly be set for you!

Formally record your targets for further development below. Make *clear* and *specific* reference to areas within your self-audit and mathematics test that require attention. Don't forget to indicate where, when and how the targets will be achieved.

Targets (areas identified from the audit and test results requiring attention)

Number	Algebra – patterns and relationships	Shape and space
Statistics	**Probability**	**Measures**
Equations and graphs	**Reasoning and proof**	

Part 7: Revision and further reading

Well done indeed for getting this far! By working through this book you are well on your way towards developing your mathematical knowledge and understanding. Having set targets, it is useful to know where to go for further subject knowledge support. This section outlines some of the possible choices.

There are many books to support the development of mathematical knowledge currently available. As a trainee teacher it is probably more appropriate to look at books written specifically to address the mathematical needs of trainees. Various books have been written to support students as they work to develop their subject knowledge. Some books look solely at subject knowledge, others attempt to place it more firmly within a classroom context. Which of these is most appropriate for you depends on your own needs when developing your subject knowledge. One book which addresses the learning within a classroom context is detailed below.

- Mooney, C. et al. (2012) *Primary Mathematics: Knowledge and Understanding* (6th edition). London: Sage/Learning Matters.

   The approach this book adopts endeavours to tackle the subject knowledge through a series of misconceptions that children may demonstrate in the classroom. The subject knowledge required by the teacher to effectively support and extend the child is then detailed. It also includes a review of research in each of the areas, as well as self-assessment questions to check understanding.

This book is supported and expanded by:

- Hansen, A. (2008) *Extending Knowledge in Practice: Primary Mathematics*. Exeter: Learning Matters.

Structured around the Primary National Strategy Framework for Mathematics, this book extends and deepens trainees' mathematics subject knowledge so that they are able to use it more actively in planning and implementing lessons.

It is also possible to buy plenty of GCSE revision texts which help develop knowledge at a similar level to that required by trainees. However, if you are just seeking to improve your knowledge in the areas outlined within this text, then a potential problem with using these books could be that the knowledge covered is not necessarily the knowledge required. In some areas it may be wider, in others more limited. If you are a little uncertain about mathematics, the format and the level might be a little intimidating. If you are more confident and just a little 'rusty' in a few areas they might be a suitable option.

A further option is to use the Internet to support your learning. Including specific website addresses in a book is rather risky as they tend to change quite regularly. Included here are a couple which are well established and were current at the time of writing.

- For help with revision at GCSE level, the BBC's Bitesize site is quite useful:

   http://www.bbc.co.uk/education/gcsebitesize/maths/index.shtml

- Considering mathematics more broadly, the Math Forum home page is a useful starting point. From here it is possible to search their Internet mathematics library for useful pages related to an incredibly diverse range of mathematical topics. It is also possible to e-mail Dr. Math with their *Ask Dr. Math* facility. Using this, any mathematical questions you have can be e-mailed to the Forum, who will endeavour to answer your question and publish the answer on the site.

http://mathforum.com/

Also, remember that study groups with other trainees can be invaluable. Choosing the most appropriate resource for your needs, setting clear, achievable targets and identifying specific time to develop your mathematical knowledge, skills and understanding will all support you as you work towards achieving all the requirements for gaining QTS and becoming a confident and successful teacher.